# The Power of Opposite Strengths®

Tommy Thomas, PhD
and
J. W. Thomas, EdD

## About the Cover

The infinity symbol represents the power of opposite strengths. The process of strengthening our relationships in so many ways is like traveling back and forth between the opposite ends of the infinity symbol.

Published by
Opposite Strengths, Inc.
PO Box 160220
Austin TX 78716-0220

www.oppositestrengths.com

First printing, July 2006.
Fourth printing, July 2011.

ISBN 978-0-9637450-2-6

To
Evelena Glasscock
And
Martha Jane Vandruff

# Table of Contents

List of Illustrations . . . . . . . . . . . . . . . . . . . .vii
Preface . . . . . . . . . . . . . . . . . . . . . . . . . . . .ix
How To Use This Book . . . . . . . . . . . . . . xiii

Introduction . . . . . . . . . . . . . . . . . . . . . . . . I

**Part I    Being Yourself**

Chapter  1    The Power of Opposite Strengths . . . . . . . 25
Chapter  2    Patterns of Strengths . . . . . . . . . . . . . . . . 37
Chapter  3    Innate Capacities . . . . . . . . . . . . . . . . . . . 91
Chapter  4    Environment . . . . . . . . . . . . . . . . . . . . . . 97
Chapter  5    Personal Choice . . . . . . . . . . . . . . . . . . 107
              Applying Opposite Strengths
              in Your Life . . . . . . . . . . . . . . . . . . . . . . .110
              Transition . . . . . . . . . . . . . . . . . . . . . . . .113

**Part II    Being Flexible**

Chapter  6    The Growth Process . . . . . . . . . . . . . . . . .117
Chapter  7    Personal Tendencies . . . . . . . . . . . . . . . . 129
Chapter  8    Polarization . . . . . . . . . . . . . . . . . . . . . . 135
Chapter  9    Personal Growth . . . . . . . . . . . . . . . . . . 149
              Applying Opposite Strengths
              in Your Life . . . . . . . . . . . . . . . . . . . . . . 175
              Transition . . . . . . . . . . . . . . . . . . . . . . . 177

## Part III    Sustained Success in Relationships

Chapter 10    Dynamics of a Creative Relationship .... 181
Chapter 11    Relationship Tendencies ............... 191
Chapter 12    Relationship Characteristics
of Each Pattern .................... 201
Chapter 13    How to Strengthen Relationships ........ 219
Applying Opposite Strengths
in Your Life. ....................... 227
Transition. ......................... 229

Partial List of Clients. ................ 230
About the Authors ................. 232
Index ............................ 234

vi

# List of Illustrations

Figure 1   Infinity Symbol Illustration . . . . . . . . . . . . . . 18
Figure 2   Four Life Forces . . . . . . . . . . . . . . . . . . . . . . 28
Figure 3   Three Pairs of Opposite Strengths . . . . . . . . 40
Figure 4   Patterns of Strengths . . . . . . . . . . . . . . . . 54–55
Figure 5   Eight Patterns of Strengths . . . . . . . . . . . 82–89
Figure 6   The Success Process. . . . . . . . . . . . . . . . . . . .119
Figure 7   Common Tendencies . . . . . . . . . . . . . . . . . . 132
Figure 8   Becoming Polarized on a Basic Strength . . . .141
Figure 9   Becoming Polarized on a Thinking
Strength . . . . . . . . . . . . . . . . . . . . . . . . . . . 143
Figure 10   Becoming Polarized on a Risking
Strength . . . . . . . . . . . . . . . . . . . . . . . . . . . 147
Figure 11   Sustained Success. . . . . . . . . . . . . . . . . . . . 172
Figure 12   A Creative Relationship . . . . . . . . . . . . . . . . 182
Figure 13   Two Father-Son Relationships . . . . . . . . . . 186
Figure 14   Supervisor-Subordinate Relationships . . . . . 187
Figure 15   Zone of Sustained Success. . . . . . . . . . . . . . 188
Figure 16   Relationship Tendencies. . . . . . . . . . . . . . . . 196
Figure 17   Dealing Creatively With Our
Relationship Tendencies. . . . . . . . . . . . . . . . 221

# Preface

This book is a newly revised version of *Your Personal Growth*, which was first published in 1971 by Frederick Fell of New York. Since that time, it has undergone several revisions and title changes. It has appeared as *Bi/Polar: A Positive Way of Understanding People* (1977), *Bi/Polar: Understanding People Through Strengths* (1985), *Bi/Polar: Foundations of Productivity* (1990), and *The Thomas Concept* (1998). This newest edition of the book, as well as the reports generated from our Web site, relied heaving on the editing skills of Dr. Lee Poynor, a psychologist and author in her own right. Patrick Owens created all new graphical illustrations for this book, our Web site, and our seminar materials. He and Stephanie Schuhmacher also designed the layout for this book. For all their excellent work, we are grateful

The original name for the Power of Opposite Strengths was the Bi/Polar® Concept. We used the registered trademark "Bi/Polar" from 1966 through 1997, and that word became strongly identified with our entire teaching endeavor. Unfortunately for us, in the early 1970's the term "bipolar" began to be used by the therapeutic community as a shorthand term for the manic-depressive personality disorder.

For many years, this was not a problem, since most lay people were not aware of "bipolar" as a therapeutic term. Then, professionals in the therapeutic community began to diagnose an increasing number of people as "bipolar." By the late 1980's, "bipolar" found its way into the vernacular of the U.S., and the identity of our entire system began to be confused with the manic-depressive disorder. At that point, hard reality forced us to abandon the term and identity we had nurtured and used for so many years. It was somewhat amusing and ironic that those who assigned "bipolar" a meaning of dysfunction usurped our original meaning of psychological health. Another interesting twist is that our willingness to give up and let go of the "bipolar" tag was a profound expression of our own belief in the core tenets of the Power of Opposite Strengths.

The newest name for our approach of using *strengths* to understand people is the Power of Opposite Strengths. We are freshening up our approach in a number of other ways, as well. Most notably, we have added a strong online presence with our continually evolving Web site, *www.oppositestrengths.com*. Dr. Hugh Poynor has been instrumental in making our Web site functional and user-friendly. His expertise in not only the technical aspects of programming and Web design but his background and experience as a psychologist have been essential elements in making the Power of Opposite Strengths what it is today.

Hand in hand with these new developments has come a renewed sense of excitement about the future. Our emphasis on understanding and teaching about human relationships (the relationship one has with oneself and the relationships one has with other people) has given us a renewed vision of what the Power of Opposite Strengths can offer the world.

Jay Thomas, the senior author, discovered the Power of Opposite Strengths. His uniquely positive way of understanding people through strengths grew out of his experiences as a management psychologist, beginning in 1955 and spanning over four decades. All of the previous books on the Power of Opposite Strengths were the results of his writing efforts and were grounded in his experiences.

Tommy Thomas, the junior author, is Jay's son. The two of us have been working together as educational and consulting psychologists and trainers since 1977. Tommy updated the original books to create this one.

We want to thank the many people who have contributed insights to the Power of Opposite Strengths over the years as well as those many clients who have used our system to our mutual benefit. Hardy Clemons, Beverly Charles, John and Judy Thompson, Jim Mayfield, Mike Horton, Robby Robinson, David Finley, Phil Kirk, Wally Vlasak, Roy and Kay Woodruff, Bob Whitten, Glynn Ford, R. D. O'Connor, Gordon Anderson, Jack Bates, Jackson Hinds, Gareth Wood, Gene Davenport, and Byron Googins come to mind immediately. In naming these few, we regrettably leave out many more. We trust that you know who you are and forgive us our oversight.

As Opposite Strengths has continued to evolve as the premier executive coaching system available in the world today, so has the primary book explaining the Opposite Strengths System. What you won't find are major upheavals in the theory and concepts as the fundamental ideas of Opposite Strengths continue to stand the test of time. We'd like to thank all our clients and especially the members of the growing Opposite Strengths Certified Executive Coach community. We are just beginning to change the mindset of the world from "strengths and weaknesses" to "opposite strengths."

T.J.T.    J.W.T.

Austin, Texas
July 2011

# How To Use This Book

This book is the "authority" for information about the Power of Opposite Strengths. Styled somewhere between a textbook and a popular self-help book, it is intended to serve as the primary source on the theoretical and philosophical foundations of the Power of Opposite Strengths.

The book will be most meaningful and useful if it is read in conjunction with attending an Opposite Strengths Seminar or Opposite Strengths Executive Coaching experience, or if it is used to enhance the insights gained through our Web site, *www.oppositestrengths.com*.

---

More information about the Opposite Strengths Seminar, our in-depth online reports, and how to contact us is available on our Web site, *www.oppositestrengths.com*. Please visit us there.

---

At the end of each of the three major sections of this book, you (the reader) will be invited to apply Opposite Strengths to your own life. Dr. Tommy Thomas will guide you step-by-step in how to enrich your reading of this book by applying the Opposite Strengths system to yourself. Participants in an Opposite Strengths Executive Coaching experience or Opposite Strengths Seminar will gain a better intellectual understanding of our system. They will also learn how to use it to become healthier, more productive human beings who are enjoying more satisfying relationships.

Opposite Strengths Culture Transformations are organization-wide implementations of Opposite Strengths to make Opposite Strengths a common language of communication among all employees. Culture Transformations usually occur in waves.

The first wave is composed of providing Opposite Strengths Executive Coaching for the top leadership. This is the usual way that we begin organizational culture transformations. Second and subsequent waves are a combination of Opposite Strengths Executive Coaching and Opposite Strengths Seminars to provide an organization-wide culture transformation program that results in all employees understanding and using the Power of Opposite Strengths to create a high performance, relationship-oriented culture. The resulting culture transformation is the ultimate goal of using Opposite Strengths in organizations.

This book can be used as a stand-alone introduction to the Opposite Strengths System, and you can definitely benefit from reading this book without executive coaching or training. We nevertheless encourage you to attend an Opposite Strengths Seminar or engage an Opposite Strengths Certified Executive Coach. That is because the experience is inherently richer. In a concentrated experience in a live setting, the concepts come alive as they simply cannot through the printed word, and afterwards they will come home to you more strongly in your everyday life.

Our Web site, *www.oppositestrengths.com*, is a pioneering effort to provide online psychological services and products. The site as it stands right now provides

- a community of people who use the Power of Opposite Strengths in their daily lives

- online administrations of our Self- and Other-Report *Opposite Strengths Inventories*

- our three personalized, in-depth reports, the *Guide to Being Yourself, Guide to Being Flexible*, and the *Relationship Guide*

- the Analysis of Strengths, which has been used by our Certified Executive Coaches and Certified Facilitators since 1970

- background information on our theory and our founders, Jay and Tommy Thomas

- descriptions of the Opposite Strengths Executive Coaching System and Opposite Strengths Seminar

- a list of our client organizations

- information on how to build Opposite Strengths into the culture of your organization

- information on how to build your own executive coaching business by joining the global Opposite Strengths Certified Executive Coach Community

We are well aware that the Internet is an evolving medium of communication, and we are dedicated to the proposition of developing our site in new and ever more effective ways in the future. We are pleased and proud of how far we have already come, and we are extremely confident that the site will serve our clients and us even better as it continues to evolve in the future. Since we want to keep the information in our printed matter as current as possible, we intentionally avoid references to those parts of our Web site that are likely to evolve much more quickly than our printed products. That is a difficult challenge.

# Introduction

## What Is an Insight?

*"The joy of insight is a sense of involvement and awe, the elated state of mind that you achieve when you have grasped some essential point; it is akin to what you feel on top of a mountain after a hard climb or when you hear a great work of music."*
—Victor Weisskopf

Webster's dictionary defines "insight" as "the ability to see and understand clearly the inner nature of things." People who discover the Power of Opposite Strengths acquire *the ability to see and understand clearly the inner nature of human relationships.*

Every human being has two kinds of relationships. These are the relationship with the self and relationships with other people. Both kinds must be strong in order for the individual to live a healthy and productive life. The Power of Opposite Strengths addresses both. If the focus of the Power of Opposite Strengths can be described in one word, that word is "relationships".

Our insights are philosophically grounded and psychologically oriented. We reach within and touch the core of the individual. Our insights create what Peter Senge, in his book *The Fifth Discipline*, calls a "mental model." This mental model creates a common language for understanding people and relationships in organizations.

In the Myers-Briggs Type Indicator, DiSC, and a multitude of other categorizing and "typing" practices, identifying people's characteristics is an end in itself. In our view, understanding one's natural characteristics is a means to a positive, endless process, not an end in itself. As you will see as you gain the insights of this book, self-facilitation of the process of using strengths is the key to personal growth, effectiveness, and a healthy relationship with oneself.

Our theory is also very different from behaviorism. Dr. B. F. Skinner taught that only what can be observed (behavior) is important, and that what affects behavior most is the environment. Although we recognize that the environment can have important influences on how we behave (see Chapter 4), our emphasis is exactly the opposite. We look *within*.

When he talks about training and development activities, one of our Canadian consulting clients uses an iceberg analogy. "Self skills" make up 90% of the iceberg—the part that is below the water and invisible. In contrast, learnable "work skills" and "technical skills" make up only the top, visible 10% of the iceberg—and are wholly supported by the self skills.

In the same vein, what is it that we admire about a beautiful tree? Imagine those huge and aged redwoods from northern California. They grow several hundred feet tall and as much as 50 feet in circumference. But what is it that makes the beautiful trunk and branches and leaves possible? It is the roots—the foundation of any tree. As with the iceberg, the foundation is hard to see—and it is even harder to tell how big it is. Its importance, however, is immediately clear. Without an extensive root system to anchor the tree to the ground and to provide life-giving sustenance to the trunk and the branches, the tree would not exist.

Quite a different analogy may speak to the millions (or billions) of people who have become dependent upon personal computers (or PCs). In order for any computer to work, it must have the right applications software—for accounting, data base management, word processing, games, and so forth. Without the correct software, the computer is nothing better than a paperweight. Underlying all of the applications software, however, is another level of essential programming: the operating system.

Historically, that was a program called DOS, for Disk Operating System. The most widely used system today, of course, is Windows. It is the foundation of the PC. Without Windows or an equivalent operating system directing traffic, none of the application programs would be able to function.

The Power of Opposite Strengths is like a Personal Operating System—a Window into the person. It is a system that helps people understand their personal foundations. It allows people to

- find their inner strengths—to know why they do the things they do

- understand how and why they are the same as and different from other people

- learn how to relate to others

- know what is innate and natural—and what requires effort and concentration to do.

A person who understands the Power of Opposite Strengths can readily draw upon that foundation to enhance other training, development, and educational activities. He or she will be able to personalize the experience, relating it to his or her own strengths and newly acquired understanding of others. Moreover, that person—whether a manager, a trainer, human resources specialist, or a member of a technical or professional team—will understand why training, development, and educational programs should not treat everyone the same nor expect everyone to benefit in the same ways from the same experiences.

## What Is Productivity?

"Productivity" has been a buzzword in the business world and in training and development circles for a number of years. It is also a term that is often tossed out rather carelessly. For us, however, it has two very specific meanings. The first has to do with personal productivity, and the second has to do with organizational productivity.

Personal productivity has to do with how well a person achieves his or her potential as an individual. More specifically, it has to do with how well a person realizes who he or she was meant to be, how to live a satisfying life, and how to develop healthy relationships with others. In a work setting, an individual is productive according to how well he or she achieves goals or completes projects that benefit the organization. This includes a primary emphasis on how well that individual relates to and communicates with others in the organization.

Organizational productivity has to do with how well an organization carries out its mission. If an organization exists to accomplish certain goals, the extent to which those goals are achieved is a measure of that organization's productivity. Many factors affect an organization's productivity: the market, economic conditions, demand for the organization's product, the availability of materials, laws, and others. Individuals within the organization also help (or hinder) the organization as it attempts to meet its stated goals.

What we focus on in our work with organizations is that sometimes overlooked but supremely important issue of how well the people in an organization are relating to one another and working together. Sometimes, factors beyond their control thwart even people who work together well, so that their personal productivity becomes a moot issue for the organization. (For example, demand for the product the company manufactures might drop, leading to plummeting sales figures.) Often, however, an organization has every other factor working in its favor and still falls short of meeting realistic goals. In that case, the people in the organization simply are not producing because of problems with relationships between people, failure to recognize individuals' abilities and strengths, and/or confusion about where the organization is headed.

The above situation is exactly what the Power of Opposite Strengths is designed to correct. The Power of Opposite Strengths can help turn an organization around and set it back on the path to organizational health and productivity. That is because the Power of Opposite Strengths improves people's skills in communicating with one another, recognizing one another's strengths, focusing on common goals, supporting one another, and working as a team to help the organization achieve its goals.

---

The foundational insights of the Power of Opposite Strengths help people to achieve both personal and organizational productivity.

---

## The Opposite Strengths Seminar

The Opposite Strengths Seminar experience that accompanies this book provides individuals with a foundation on which they can structure more productive and satisfying lives. People who attend and gain insights into their own unique personal make-ups leave the event equipped to make choices that result in personal growth and increased productivity. Better yet, the insights they carry away will literally last them for the rest of their lives. (Visit *www.oppositestrengths.com* for more information about how you can attend an Opposite Strengths Seminar.)

The Opposite Strengths Seminar rests on the solid bedrock of a fundamental concept—an idea regarding the basic nature of what makes us a creative and living species. This concept has undergirded and pervaded the seminar since its inception in 1966. It is the strong anchor point of the entire

Opposite Strengths System for understanding the spectrum of human relationships.

The Power of Opposite Strengths is a marvelously simple idea, but at the same time it contains one of the most profound truths about life and existence. At first blush, the simplicity of the concept may cause one to miss the deep meaning that is within it. The depth of the idea is usually revealed over time, as one has the opportunity to apply it to different situations and reflect upon its fundamental truth.

A simple statement of the Power of Opposite Strengths is that creativity and productivity are the results of a process in which two opposite strengths are interacting together and contributing equally to the process. This is in contrast with the view that two opposites are inherently in conflict, with one being more valuable than the other.

An example should help clarify these two different conceptions. Consider the two strengths thinking (reason) and risking (action). People commonly tend to regard these two opposite strengths as being in conflict with one another and to believe that one is more important or valuable than the other. Some consider thinking to be more valuable, while others consider risking being more valuable. The Power of Opposite Strengths establishes quite a different view of these two strengths. Thinking and risking are believed to complement each other and to have equal intrinsic value as they interact with each other creatively. Even more explicitly, thinking and risking are seen as two complementary strengths that work together as equal partners to produce individual and organizational productivity.

Throughout, the Opposite Strengths Seminar is firmly grounded in the bedrock of the Power of Opposite Strengths. It is organized around four areas of understanding that form the foundation for personal and organizational development:

- understanding and appreciating ourselves
- understanding and experiencing the growth process
- understanding and appreciating other people
- understanding and strengthening our relationships with others.

The first part of the Opposite Strengths Seminar focuses on understanding and appreciating oneself.

## Being Yourself

We use the Power of Opposite Strengths to help us understand and appreciate who we are at the core of our being. Your relationship with yourself affects all other aspects of your life, including your relationships with others. The system itself has evolved out of working with normal, healthy people rather than people who are in the need of therapy. Our approach is positive. It allows people to understand themselves in terms of their strengths rather than their weaknesses—to learn what is creative and good about them rather than what is wrong with them. The seminar does deal with normal human tendencies that get us into trouble and cause us problems, but this comes later in the event when we take up the matter of how people express their opposite strengths.

High productivity and robust self-development require us to be ourselves—to be natural and express our own unique blend of opposite strengths. We refer to this as having a healthy relationship with ourselves. We know who we are, and we accept ourselves fully. In turn, our ability to be ourselves depends upon

- our understanding of who we really are in terms of our strengths

- the extent to which we have positive, accepting feelings towards ourselves.

A rational and reality-based understanding of ourselves helps us to know when we are being ourselves and when we are being phony. An awareness of who we really are gives us practical and concrete guidance as we seek to find those situations in which we feel at home. It helps us to identify the work situation that fits us best—where we can be the most productive and make our greatest contribution. The increased self-understanding developed in the first part of the seminar helps those who attend to be themselves more fully in the real world.

Our feelings of self-worth are also important in determining our ability to be ourselves. If we have low self-esteem and tend to view ourselves in a negative way, it makes it difficult for us to be ourselves. If we feel that we are somehow bad, inferior, or unacceptable, we tend to hide who we really are and try to be something different from our natural selves.

The Power of Opposite Strengths and its underlying philosophies provide a logical way of looking at ourselves in terms of our strengths. It gives us a rational basis for understanding ourselves as good at the core and equally as acceptable as everyone else regardless of what others may think. This approach tends to yield a positive, accepting attitude towards both ourselves and other people.

In the first part of the seminar, we help each participant

- build a solid foundation of self-understanding that is based on strengths
- develop healthy, reality-based attitudes of self-affirmation.

In the second part of the Opposite Strengths Seminar, we focus upon the process through which we all grow and become stronger and more productive individuals—by learning how to be flexible.

## Being Flexible

As we build our foundation for personal development, it is essential that we understand what flexibility really is. We use the Power of Opposite Strengths as the central tool to deepen our understanding of what is actually going on in the process of flexibility, which is the underlying process of personal growth.

In addition to understanding the growth process itself, it is equally important that we understand how we as individuals relate to this process. In the Opposite Strengths system, we assume that every person participates naturally in the growth process. We also assume that we can get out of the process either through the influence of a negative environment or through making wrong personal choices. Our task in this part of the seminar is to understand those forces that tend to take us out of the growth process and to identify the personal choices we must make to stay in it.

In the first part of the seminar, we say that being ourselves is essential for self-development. We say this in spite of the realization that in being ourselves we will experience problems with the world. In this part, we introduce an equally important requirement for growth: We must solve the problems that we create by being ourselves.

We solve these problems by emphasizing the strengths that are the opposites of those that we normally emphasize when we are being ourselves. When we make this shift of emphasis, we usually feel awkward and uncomfortable and can even feel as if we are not being ourselves.

Some people, for example, naturally express more independence than dependence on others. (In the Opposite Strengths

System, independence and dependence are opposite and equally valuable strengths.) As a result of their natural emphasis on independence, they are less reliant on their dependence. This can cause problems, particularly in their relationships. They must solve those problems by consciously becoming more dependent on others. Emphasizing their dependent strength will feel clumsy and unnatural, but that is what is required if they are to grow and become more productive and mature individuals.

Understanding the growth process and knowing what we must do to experience personal growth in our own lives are essential for personal development and developing a healthy relationship with ourselves.

## Sustained Success in Relationships

In the first two parts of the seminar, we are guided to look within—to discover who we really are as unique, one-of-a-kind individuals and to understand what we must do, as individuals, to grow and become more productive. Then we are ready to direct our attention outward—toward other people and our relationships with them.

The third part of the seminar deals first with understanding and appreciating others. Here, we use the Power of Opposite Strengths in much the same way that we used it to understand and appreciate ourselves. The difference is that we focus on other people rather than ourselves.

The Power of Opposite Strengths helps us to understand other people as they really are—to understand how they are put together at the core of their being. We come to understand that we are all the same in that we have the same human strengths, but we are different in that we tend to favor different strengths. Understanding the strengths that a particular person tends to favor goes a long way in helping us to understand that individual as a person.

Becoming aware of other people's favored strengths not only helps us to understand them in terms of their strengths, but it also helps us to understand why they think and behave in the way they do—which may be very different from how we ourselves behave. It helps us to understand their natural tendencies and gives us a better appreciation of the problems and growth challenges they tend to experience.

The understanding and appreciation we develop for other people in this part of the seminar, coupled with our own self-understanding and appreciation, lays the groundwork for the attitudes and behaviors that are essential for developing strong and productive relationships with other people. The last part of the seminar deals directly with how we go about strengthening our relationships and improving our communication with others.

Other approaches to understanding the dynamics of human relationships tend to shy away from attitudes and focus on behaviors. We regard this as a mistake. In our system, we consider attitude and behavior to be equally important in determining the quality of our relationships.

The two essential ingredients in a creative relationship are

- having an attitude of equality

- appropriately blending assertive and reserved behavior.

We communicate an attitude of equality to other people when we...

- value them as much as we value ourselves

- look straight across at them—not up to or down on them

- are equally as concerned with our welfare and theirs

- have self-respect as well as respect for them

- take equal responsibility for making our relationship work

- focus as much attention on them as on ourselves.

To the extent that we deviate from an attitude of equality, we lose the potential creativeness of the relationship. Two common attitudes—self-focused and others-focused—can become destructive to our relationships. We tend to communicate a self-focused attitude when we consistently pay more attention to ourselves than to the other person—when we are more concerned with our own wants, needs, and desires than with those of the other person. We tend to communicate an others-focused attitude when we consistently pay more attention to the other person than we do to ourselves—when we are more concerned with the wants, needs, and desires of other persons than we are with our own.

During this part of the seminar, we help participants become aware of the attitude they tend to communicate in their relationships. We also give them guidance on how to develop and communicate an attitude of equality.

Being assertive and being reserved are the two opposite kinds of behavior that are blended in a creative relationship. The appropriate blend of these two behaviors is determined by the core characteristics of the two people involved *and* the particular situation in which they find themselves. While the attitude of equality remains constant regardless of the situation or the differing characteristics of the two people, the appropriate blend of behavior is a dynamic, changing combination that is continually modified and adjusted to fit the situation.

Understanding ourselves and understanding the other person are both critical for determining the appropriate behavior in a relationship with a particular person. At this point in the seminar, we draw heavily on the understandings of others and ourselves that were developed in the earlier part of the program.

In fact, the entire seminar builds upon itself. First, we deepen our understanding and appreciation of ourselves. Next, we develop an understanding of flexibility and the growth process, which leads us to experience a productive relationship with ourselves. Finally, we develop a deeper understanding and appreciation of the unique individuality of every other person. These insights are then used to help us understand what is going on in our relationships with others and what we need to do to strengthen them.

Many people who have attended the Opposite Strengths Seminar report that the greatest practical value of the seminar experience has been helping them to understand and strengthen their relationships with others. On the other hand, many people have felt that the insights they developed into their relationships with themselves have been the most rewarding personally.

# The Power of Opposite Strengths

*"The test of a first-rate intelligence is the ability to hold two opposed ideas in the mind at the same time and still retain the ability to function."*

—F. SCOTT FITZGERALD

The whole Opposite Strengths System hangs on this one simple idea:  that sustained success comes from the blending of two opposite strengths.

The first step in Jay Thomas's own awareness of the concept came from his recognition that there were two distinct types of company presidents. Both were successful, yet they were very different. In fact, in many ways they were exact opposites. One type of president tended to be dynamic, enthusiastic, and action-oriented and seemed to have a natural propensity toward risk taking. The other type tended to be stable, analytical, and well

organized. Unlike the risk-taking presidents, they seemed to
have a propensity for thoughtful analysis. Both types could be
successful as a chief executive officer of a company, and invariably, both types would develop problems that stemmed directly from their natural bent towards either dynamic action or
thoughtful analysis.

Companies that had dynamic, self-confident, action-oriented
presidents tended to develop problems associated with quick
decisions, lack of sufficient planning, lack of organization, and a
need for stability, efficiency, and control. The activity and movement resulting from their dynamic, risk-taking strengths were an
essential part of the company's growth—but only a part. The other part needed to come from opposite and balancing strengths—
the stable thinking strengths.

Some of the action-oriented presidents had an appreciation
for the value of the thinking strengths and found effective ways to
incorporate thoughtful analyses into their decision-making. The
presidents who did this tended to build strong and growing companies. Their companies maintained their basic orientation towards
action and dynamism but became stronger and more successful by
blending in more rational analysis and thoughtful planning.

In those instances where the dynamic president failed to
make these thinking strengths a greater force in the management
of the company, things became progressively worse. The organization seemed to go into a spiral of decay. Rather than solving
problems by using more of their thinking strengths, they tried to
solve them by becoming even more active and taking even greater risks. As a result, more and more bad decisions were made.
Operational problems compounded and caused even greater
inefficiencies. Financial problems loomed larger and larger and
threatened the existence of the company. At some point in this
decay process, one of two things usually happened: either the

company declared bankruptcy, or it was taken over by a stronger and more stable company.

The stable, thought-oriented presidents were, in many ways, opposite from the dynamic entrepreneurs—and they developed opposite kinds of problems. Their natural leaning toward thinking and planning brought stability, structure, and efficiency to their organizations. These are valuable and essential strengths in any strong and growing organization, but they are only a part of its creative growth. The other part comes from dynamic, action-oriented strengths—the very strengths that characterized the more dynamic presidents.

Organizations led by these conservative, thinking-oriented leaders tended to develop a need for stronger expressions of the dynamic strengths. The companies' growth was inhibited because of a lack of decision, a lack of action, and a need for more dynamism. In some instances, the thought-oriented presidents recognized the values of the dynamic, action-oriented strengths and found effective ways to make these strengths a stronger part of their organizations. When they did this, they created stronger and more dynamically growing companies. Their organizations remained stable and well organized, but the introduction of more dynamism made them more active, aggressive, and profitable.

In those instances where the dynamic strengths were not brought in, the organizations tended to become stagnant and die on the vine. They entered their own spiral of decay characterized by indecisiveness, weak commitments, and boring inactivity. Management tried to solve these problems by doing even more thinking, rather than getting into action and taking more risks. As the decay process progressed, these companies either gradually withered away or were taken over by more aggressive and dynamic companies.

These experiences and insights are what originally put Jay Thomas on the track of the Power of Opposite Strengths. It made sense to him that growth would naturally come from strengths—not from weaknesses. As a result, he focused on strengths from the very beginning. He felt his challenge was to identify the strengths that produce growth and to understand how these strengths relate to each other. In trying to meet that challenge, he gradually formulated the six principles presented below. Taken together, they constitute the essential features of the Power of Opposite Strengths.

# First Principle
### *A strength is non-productive by itself.*

Although each strength is positive in its fundamental nature, it must blend with its opposite in order to produce growth. Productivity comes from a blend and interaction of two opposite strengths, not from one strength alone.

# Second Principle
### *Each of the two opposite strengths involved in the process is wholly positive—neither is negative.*

The two opposite strengths in each pair are inherently positive, because each makes its own positive contribution to the creative growth process. Neither strength should ever be regarded as weak or intrinsically negative. A strength can be expressed at an inappropriate time, but this does not make it negative in and of itself. Any negative quality stems from the inappropriate use of the strength—not from the strength itself.

# Third Principle

***The opposite strengths in each pair contribute equally to the growth process.***

The strengths in each pair are inherently equal. Although they are opposites and contribute different values, their contributions are of equal worth and value to the whole. It is important to recognize that we are referring to the intrinsic value of the two strengths with respect to the total process—not to an immediate need within a particular situation. A particular situation may require more of one of the strengths to stimulate growth, but this immediate need for an emphasis on one of the strengths does not make that strength inherently more valuable to the process itself. The opposite strength will need to be emphasized at a later time.

# Fourth Principle

***The expression of one strength creates a need for the expression of its opposite strength.***

As one strength is used, a consequent need for the expression of its opposite strength builds in the individual. The need for this expression builds over time and is alleviated only by the expression of the opposite strength.

# Fifth Principle

***Opposite strengths support and feed each other.***

Although two opposite strengths (such as thought and action) may sometimes appear to be in conflict, they actually support and feed one another. In the growth process, they have a reciprocal, interdependent, synergistic relationship. Each gives to and takes from the other.

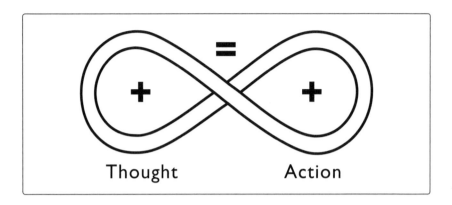

*Figure 1*

They key to this understanding was the realization that the activity of a strength always takes place within the context of its opposite and always produces a result. This insight laid the foundation for understanding how the opposite strengths actually relate to each other in the creative growth process. The relationship may be described in the following way.

Exercising a strength results in a product which, in turn, becomes the raw material that is used by its opposite in the production of its own result. In other words, each strength is dependent upon the activity of its opposite to provide the raw material it needs to produce its own result. This is an ongoing process that can be likened to a continuous feedback loop.

A real-world example should be useful in clarifying this concept. As discussed earlier, the opposite strengths that were found to differentiate between the two basic types of corporate presidents are thought and action. The thinking strengths of the thought-oriented presidents produced well-thought-out strategies and plans. The risking strengths of the action-oriented presidents produced the drive and courage to get into action and do things. In the creative growth of a company, these two opposite strengths work together and feed into each other. The thinking strength produces the strategies for creative action, which serve as input for the risking strength. The risking strength drives the implementation of those strategies. The evident results of the action taken become new data upon which the thinking strength operates to fine-tune or develop new plans and strategies. Each strength fuels the other, and both become more productive in the process. They are synergistic.

# Sixth Principle
**_Growth is a process in which two opposite strengths interact with one another._**

This hypothesis points to the inherent duality of the fundamental forces that power the growth process. Growth and creativity are conceived as being expressed in pairs of strengths—always two opposite strengths. The two strengths in each pair are opposite to each other in much the same way that the North and South Poles are opposite to each other as well as being essential parts of a common entity The same is true of the pairs of strengths within people—they are opposites, yet both are essential parts of one process.

The infinity symbol drawn in Figure 1 may be used to review and illustrate the six principles that undergird the Power of Opposite Strengths. The two loops in the symbol may be used to represent the two opposite strengths in a pair. In this drawing, we are using a basic pair that is well understood—thought and action—but one needs to keep in mind that there are other pairs of opposite strengths.

By tracing the outline of the symbol back and forth, we can illustrate the first principle that (1) growth is a process in which thought and action interact with each other. By placing an equals sign between the two loops, we can indicate that (2) thought and action have equal value in the process. By placing a plus sign above each of the two loops, we signify that (3) both strengths are inherently positive. By blocking out one of the loops, we can also show that (4) either thought or action is nonproductive by itself. Finally, by tracing the outline of the symbol back and forth, we can indicate how (5) thought and action feed and support each other.

The six principles evolved gradually over a period of years. This is especially true of the insight described under the fifth principle, that the activity of a strength always produces a result in the context of its opposite. That realization occurred at least 10 years after the first awareness of the Power of Opposite Strengths.

Succinctly put, the Power of Opposite Strengths can be stated as follows.

**Creativity and growth come from a blending of two opposite strengths. Each of these two strengths makes its own positive contribution to the process, and they are equal partners in the creative whole formed by their interaction.**

It is difficult to overemphasize the fundamental importance of the simple idea that we call the Power of Opposite Strengths. It is central and essential to understanding the Power of Opposite Strengths system.

## Summary

In this Introduction, we have explained the six principles of the Power of Opposite Strengths, the structure of the book, and the benefits you and your organization can expect from using the Power of Opposite Strengths as a tool for developing people. The remainder of the book is devoted to the substance of the Power of Opposite Strengths and the benefits you can expect to receive from understanding and using it.

At the end of each of the three major sections of the book, Dr. Tommy Thomas shows how you can incorporate a learning experience for yourself into the progress you are making in reading this book. You can actually think of reading this book as part of an online, self-paced, self-directed, personal seminar. In the later chapters, we will also show you how you can get others involved in this experience with you.

# PART I
## Being Yourself

# 1

# The Power of Opposite Strengths

This chapter presents the philosophical and theoretical foundations of the Power of Opposite Strengths. It is divided into two sections. The first, called *Basic Assumptions*, develops the philosophical base on which the system is built. The second, *Four Personality Forces*, presents our theory regarding the nature of the human personality and how it is formed.

## Basic Assumptions

Any effort to establish a sound theoretical base for a psychological system eventually leads to fundamental questions regarding the source of life and the human being's relationship to this source. What is the nature of the primordial force that creates all existence? What is the relationship between this force and human beings? What does this relationship say about the basic nature of human beings? What follows is an attempt to answer these questions.

In the Power of Opposite Strengths, a fundamental assumption is that there is one primordial force out of which all existence and meaning comes into being. It is a unity in that nothing exists outside it. It is a duality in that it manifests itself in pairs of opposite forces.

This primordial force is thought to be creative in its most fundamental nature, with its creativity arising out of the balanced interaction of the opposite forces that constitute its being. These opposing forces are viewed as positive strengths that interact in pairs, with each strength making its own particular contribution to the creative whole. In essence, this primordial force is seen as wholly positive.

A second fundamental assumption is that human beings (along with all entities in the world) are created and sustained by this one primordial force. We enjoy our existence and live our lives as a part of the creative process powered by this unified primordial force. All that we are and will ever be comes from the creative interaction of these primordial, opposite forces.

What do these assumptions about the source of our existence and our relationship to it have to do with the Power of Opposite Strengths? They provide the foundation for our psychological system. They establish a particular view regarding the basic nature of human beings, and this view becomes the cornerstone of the Power of Opposite Strengths. Specifically, it means that our approach is based on the assumption that human nature is grounded in strengths—not in weaknesses! We are naturally creative, and our task is to find ways to release this creative potential. This makes the Power of Opposite Strengths a positive psychology that sees strengths rather than weaknesses—what is right about a person rather than what is wrong.

That said, the Power of Opposite Strengths is definitely not a "Pollyanna psychology"—meaning one that refuses to look at the reality of the problems and pains we all experience. Our approach recognizes and affirms the reality of destructive forces in the world but views the creative forces as more fundamental. The negative, destructive force comes from our inappropriate *use* of a strength, not from the strength itself.

Our position is that our natural strengths, which come from the creative force in the universe, are the very essence of our being, while the problems, pains, and frustrations we experience are more peripheral. Describing these negatives as "peripheral" does not in any way lessen their importance in our lives or deny their reality. It does, however, establish their relationship to our creative strengths. Another way to describe this relationship is to say that whenever we have a problem or a pain, we can be confident that we have a positive strength within us that is more fundamental and has the inherent power to overcome and solve the problem.

# Four Life Forces

Personality refers to the total person—who we are as a result of all the influences that contribute to our development. The Power of Opposite Strengths is based upon a theory regarding these influences and the role they play in forming our personality.

The Power of Opposite Strengths postulates that human beings are created through interaction of two basic, polar-opposite forces within the unified primordial force that creates the universe. These opposite forces are

- a stabilizing force that creates structure
- a dynamic force that creates change.

In the creation of an individual personality, these two basic forces find expression in four distinct and identifiable personality forces. Two give stability to the personality, and two produce personality change.

The stabilizing force is expressed in our personality through the genetic structures underlying (1) our pattern of strengths and (2) our innate capacities. The dynamic force is expressed through the changes produced by the forces in (3) our environment and (4) our personal choices. (See Figure 2.)

# Four Life Forces

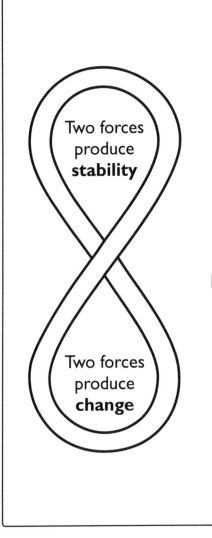

Two forces produce **stability**

Two forces produce **change**

I. **Pattern of Strengths**
Natural way of being
Basic inclinations
Inborn tendencies

II. **Innate Capacities**
Basic mental capacities
Inborn drive or energy level
Individual talents and aptitudes

III. **Environment**
Influences from other people
Social and cultural values
Effects of nutrition, injury, or illness

IV. **Personal Choices**
Conscious awareness
Deliberate actions
Personal responsibility

*Figure 2*

The laws of heredity and genetics govern our pattern of strengths and our innate capacities. This makes them stable and enduring forces in our own personality. Despite a changing environment and our flexibility to make personal choices, these forces retain their indelible imprint on our personality. Because these forces and their underlying structures within us are genetically based, certain of our personality characteristics tend to remain the same.

The two forces that allow for change in our personality are our environment and our personal choices. Different environments can produce different attitudes. For example, if a young person of high intelligence (which is a hereditary trait) is deprived of rewarding educational experiences early in life, he or she will be less likely to develop an interest in learning and reading than if exposed to a rich educational environment. The level of intelligence or capacity for learning remains constant in any one individual (innate capacity), but the attitude towards learning can be drastically different (through exposure to different environments). The other dynamic force—personal choice or free will—reflects our ability to control our own lives by conscious choice. For example, a person can overcome bad experiences in school and develop a healthy attitude toward learning simply by wanting to learn and consciously working toward that goal.

In the Power of Opposite Strengths, all four forces are regarded as inherently of equal importance as determinants of human personality. In the life of an actual person, however, the influence of each force is unequal. Any one of the forces can be the dominant influence in a particular person's life. For example, some people are more greatly affected by significant personal experiences (environment), while others may be guided most by significant personal talents (innate capacities). Also, the relative influence of these forces may be different at different times in any one person's life. At times, personal choice may be the significant force that shapes the personality. At other times, environment may have more of an impact.

The essential point is that for any particular person at any given time

- all of the forces are having some influence

- any one of the forces may be the dominant influence.

In our attempt to understand ourselves and other people, we cannot afford to depreciate or disregard any of the four fundamental forces.

Psychologists are often asked, "Are people basically the same, or is each of us unique?" The answer to this question is paradoxical, since there is an element of truth in both possible answers. The answer closest to the truth incorporates both: People are basically the same *and* they are unique.

Another frequently asked question is, "Do we remain basically the same during our lives, or do we change?" Again, the answer is paradoxical: We stay the same *and* we change. Any attempt to resolve the paradox in favor of one side or the other takes us farther from the truth.

## Pattern of Strengths

At conception, an individual is created with a particular pattern of strengths—opposite strengths that come from the primordial creative force in the universe. Although all individuals have a common humanity in that they participate in the same strengths, they are different in that they participate in these strengths in different ways.

This cluster of strengths within every individual is integrally involved in the creative process—and it makes every person a participant in the creativeness of the universe. It is a person's foundation of productivity.

Moreover, we are made entirely of strengths. There is nothing weak, evil, or destructive within our core. The Power of Opposite Strengths provides no basis on which to judge the value of one cluster as compared to another. Since we have no standard for judging one strength to be better than another, the clusters are regarded as equally important and valuable. At the core, there is no such thing as a misfit or an inferior person.

In understanding this cluster of internal strengths, the Power of Opposite Strengths recognizes three pairs of interrelated, opposite strengths. The three pairs are a basic pair (thinking/risking) and two additional pairs that come out of the basic pair—a thinking pair (practical/ theoretical) and a risking pair (dependent/independent). All of these opposite strengths are positive in their basic nature and contribute to the creative process at work in the world. They have equal value to one another, and all are required in the process of creation.

The Power of Opposite Strengths recognizes that each person has a lead strength and a supporting strength in each of the three pairs. When a lead strength is identified in each pair, it yields a particular pattern of strengths. This procedure results in eight possible combinations of three lead strengths, or eight distinctive patterns of strengths. These are the personal foundations of productivity from which we operate as individuals.

The eight patterns of strengths are the basic tools used in the Power of Opposite Strengths for understanding how we express our strengths. A good understanding of each pattern and an appreciation for its distinctiveness is critical for any effective use of our approach. Since much of the development work in the Power of Opposite Strengths has focused on the pattern of strengths, much of what the system has to offer comes from its contribution to understanding this force as a part of our lives.

The pattern of strengths discussed above refers to a configuration of relative strengths within a person. No attempt is made to measure its magnitude compared to any outside standard. People do differ, however, in how much strength they have compared with one another. The term "innate capacities" is used to point to this additional way in which we differ.

## Innate Capacities

Through the years, many psychologists have attempted to identify and measure individual differences. Much progress has been made—particularly in measuring various kinds of mental abilities. The Power of Opposite Strengths does affirm the validity of individual differences in innate capacities and recognizes the importance of considering them in any attempt truly to understand an individual as a unique person.

The critical point to recognize is that we are referring to two separate and distinct forces when we use the terms "pattern of strengths" and "innate capacities." The pattern of strengths is a particular configuration of relative strengths within a person. It says nothing about how much strength we have compared with other people. On the other hand, measures of innate capacities describe how much strength individuals have in comparison with other people and say nothing about people's internal patterns of strengths.

## Environment

External environment is the third of the four important forces that interact with each other to produce an authentic human being. We believe that the emphasis that has been placed on this force—particularly by social scientists—has tended to exaggerate the importance of the environment and depreciate the importance of the other three forces. Many people, including many psychologists, tend to believe that environment is consistently the most influential force in determining how we express our strengths.

The Power of Opposite Strengths rejects this view and maintains that all four of the life forces discussed here have equal status. None is consistently more important than the others. Environment may be the dominant force at a particular time in a person's life, and it may be the most influential overall force in a particular person's life, but the same can be said of any of the other three forces, as well!

A great number of professionally competent people have made valuable contributions to our understanding of the effects of environment on the formation of the human personality. Those of us who use the Power of Opposite Strengths do not seek to depreciate the contributions made by those who emphasize the importance of environment. We use their concepts and insights with deep gratitude and a keen appreciation for their value. All the Power of Opposite Strengths calls for is that all four of the personality forces be given equal consideration when we are trying to understand a particular person.

Environmental forces influence people in important ways. Environment is unquestionably a major factor in conceptual and emotional learning. Our value system, our attitudes, our prejudices, and our knowledge of the world come largely from people around us. At the same time, the influence of our environment is limited—by the other three forces. The same is true for the other three life forces, as well: Each is limited by the other forces. Specifically, the effects of environment are limited by the stabilizing forces within the genetic structures that underlie a person's internal pattern of strengths and innate capacities. Our power to make personal choices regarding how we respond to our environment is the third factor limiting the influence of environment on people.

As with its treatment of innate capacities, the Power of Opposite Strengths does not focus on the effects of the environment in the formation of personality. Many professionals focus on the environment as a force, and much can be learned from their work. Our emphasis in the Power of Opposite Strengths, however, is on the first and last forces of the four identified forces—the pattern of strengths and personal choice.

## Personal Choice

The final life force is referred to as personal choice—our power to make conscious choices in how we think and how we behave. These choices make a difference in who we become as unique personalities.

Our personal freedom to make conscious choices is the last of the four forces to come into being. In the beginning, an individual is created with a particular pattern of strengths and particular amounts of innate capacities. Laws of genetics and inheritance are in operation here. Immediately after conception, the environment surrounding the individual begins to influence how and to what extent the basic pattern and innate capacities are expressed. This influence begins in the womb, is dramatically expanded at birth, and continues throughout the lifetime of the individual. As the strengths within the individual interact and feed each other, conscious awareness eventually comes into being. Our power to make personal choices is born at the instant personal consciousness becomes a reality. Conscious awareness creates our freedom to choose.

We do not choose personal freedom—it is thrust upon us. It comes to us through the unconscious creative interaction of the strengths within us. Although we are not accountable for the existence of our personal freedom, we are accountable for its use once it is there. How we choose to think and act makes a difference, both in our own lives and the lives of those we touch.

As is true with the other three personality forces, our personal freedom is limited. Not only is our personal freedom limited in some important and obvious ways by the environment, but also by the stable forces expressed through the genetic structures underlying our pattern of strengths and our innate capacities. Our pattern and our innate capacities are stable features of our personality: They keep their biological structures regardless of how we choose to think and behave. Through conscious choice, we can influence how our basic pattern and our innate capacities are expressed, but this does not involve a change in our natural way of being or our innate capacities.

A constant objective in the development of the Power of Opposite Strengths has been to identify what people can and cannot do about their own personal growth. Much of what the Power of Opposite Strengths has to offer comes through its concepts of how we can consciously use our power of personal choice to express our strengths in creative ways—ways that are in harmony with the creative process at work in the world.

# 2

# Patterns of Strengths

The Power of Opposite Strengths gives us the opportunity to describe the core of one's personality in terms of process-oriented, positive strengths—with no negatives. The resultant framework allows us to understand how our strengths to the other three forces that influence the formation of the human personality.

As mentioned earlier, the Power of Opposite Strengths focuses on two of the life forces that produce a complete person—our pattern of strengths and our freedom to make personal choices. This chapter deals with the first of these forces—our pattern of strengths. We will review the basic nature of the pattern of strengths, identify the strengths that constitute it, describe how these opposite strengths relate to one another, show how eight distinctive patterns are formed, describe the personality characteristics produced by each of these patterns, and discuss how we can discover our own natural patterns.

## Nature of Our Pattern of Strengths

A pattern of strengths is a structured and dynamic cluster of interacting, opposite strengths at the core of every personality. This ever-present force helps to shape each individual's unique personality. In the Power of Opposite Strengths, we make the *a priori* assumption that this natural pattern does, in fact, exist within every person. The following five principles describe its basic nature.

1. The pattern of strengths is wholly positive. It is composed of interacting, opposite strengths that come from the primordial creative force that forms all existence. Whatever may be considered as negative, bad, weak, or destructive about a person is not in this natural pattern of strengths. To the extent that these negatives exist, they are found in some of the other forces that shape our lives but not in our strengths.

2. The pattern of strengths has a unique structure that remains constant throughout one's lifetime. This natural pattern of strengths is genetically based. Its unique structure is established at conception and maintains the same structure as long as the individual lives. It is the constant thread of self-identity that runs through all the changes and variability that every person experiences throughout a lifetime. The pattern of strengths is the personal foundation from which a person experiences life to the fullest.

3. The pattern of strengths is dynamic and continuously active. The opposite strengths in the natural pattern are active as long as the individual lives. The pattern's expression may be blocked or distorted by environmental forces and personal choices made by an individual, but it is always there as a constant force seeking to express itself. The pattern of strengths can be regarded as the force that gives the flavor to everyone's personality. It is basic and permeates our every thought and action. It gives form and structure to our natural way of being.

4. The pattern of strengths has the same potential to influence a person's thinking and behavior as the other three life forces. Our pattern of strengths is always influencing our thoughts and actions to some extent, but its actual influence at any particular time is variable. It varies with different

individuals, and it varies at different times within the same individual. With some people, the pattern of strengths may be the dominant force that has shaped their personality. With others, it may have had the least influence. Within a particular person, the influence will vary depending upon the particular situation and the personal choices made by that person.

5. The pattern of strengths is a way of understanding that basic paradox about people—that we are all the same and yet we are all unique. We all share in the same strengths at the core of our beings, but we experience and use them in our own unique ways.

# Three Pairs of Opposite Strengths

The pattern of strengths is composed of three pairs of opposite strengths. The basic pair is thinking and risking. Two additional pairs are obtained by identifying two opposite kinds of thinking and two opposite kinds of risking. The two opposite thinking strengths are practical thinking and theoretical thinking. The two opposite risking strengths are dependent risking and independent risking. (See Figure 3.)

Although the three pairs of strengths are interrelated in this way, they are expressed independently of one another in one's pattern of strengths. That is, if you know your lead strength in one of the pairs, it does not in anyway predict what your lead strength may be in another pair. The independence of these three pairs of strengths was first demonstrated in research presented in the *Manual for the Bi/Polar Inventory of Strengths*, 1978. These results were later confirmed in research reported by Dr. Tommy Thomas in his 1982 doctoral dissertation, *Self-Other Agreement*

# Three Pairs of Opposite Strengths

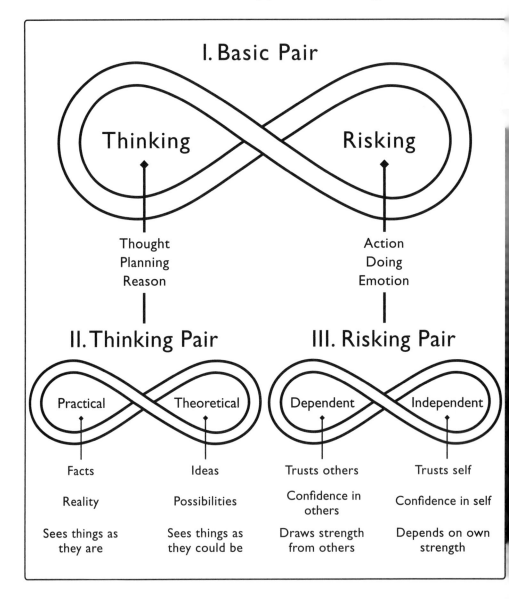

*Figure 3*

*as Manifested by Differential Responses on Self-Report and Other-Report Forms of Personality Inventories.*

## The Basic Pair—Thinking/Risking

First, we will consider the two basic strengths—thinking and risking. We all know about these two strengths because we experience them every day. We think, we feel; we plan, and we do. We analyze a problem, and we do something about it. We try to understand, and we get involved. We see other people expressing the same two strengths. They study, make decisions, try to figure things out, and take chances. They think about what to do, and they move into action. Every person has both of these strengths—a thinking strength and a risking strength.

In Jay Thomas's first attempt to classify the two basic strengths, he used "reason" and "emotion" as the two defining terms, with reason pointing toward the thinking, rational, stable side, and emotion pointing toward the risking, action, dynamic side. Before long, however, he discovered that he had made a bad choice in using the word "emotion." Although he was viewing both sides as positive strengths, he had chosen a word for the dynamic side that many people found to be negatively loaded. One executive reacted by saying, "What do you mean, emotion is a strength? That's what we want to get rid of—or, at least, control. Emotions are what cause most of our problems around here." It was obvious that a more suitable word was needed to describe the dynamic side—one that would more clearly identify that side as a strength, not as a weakness or a negative.

During the search for a more positive word to take the place of "emotion," Jay happened to be reading Paul Tillich's book, *The Courage to Be.* It quickly became apparent to Jay that Tillich was writing about the same strength Jay was trying to identify with the word "emotion," but that Tillich was using a much better word. As that point Jay started using the word "courage" to describe the strength on the emotional side. He found the switch to be very helpful. In addition to deepening his own grasp of a strength he was trying to understand, it also gave him a term that had positive rather than negative connotations. Although we still employ "courage" as one of several descriptive terms for the strength on the dynamic side, over the years "risking" has become our most commonly used term.

Our thinking strength is a stabilizing strength. It allows us to understand where we are and see where we are going. Through our thinking strength, we can plan, reason, and figure things out on a logical, analytical basis. It makes it possible for us to evaluate, weigh, and judge. It gives us the ability to visualize goals and develop strategies to reach them. Our thought processes lend stability and structure to our lives. Essentially, our thinking strength is our cognitive side.

Our risking strength is a dynamic strength. It is the wellspring of our emotional, feeling, affective side. It is an active, moving, doing kind of strength that is sometimes associated with the heart or the gut. It provides us with the courage to risk, to expose, to move out, to make a change, to initiate, to be involved, and to cause things to happen, in spite of the risk.

Both thinking and risking are happening in our lives at all times. They do so unevenly, however. Sometimes our thinking strength is most active. At other times, the reverse is true, and our risking is more active than our thinking. Someone who is sitting at a desk writing a book is focused on thinking: He or she is thinking more than risking. This does not mean that the person's risking strength is inactive, though. It is still being used, but it is in a subordinate role, supporting the thinking strength. When that same person submits a finished manuscript to a publisher in spite of the possibility of having it rejected, he or she is calling mostly on the risking strength. Certainly, both strengths are constantly active, but one or the other is always in the foreground.

We think and we risk, and we continually shift emphasis from one to the other. In addition, each of us feels more at home and comfortable expressing one of them than the other. In other words, we naturally favor either thinking or risking. It is much like being right-handed or left-handed: We are naturally inclined one way or the other out of our basic nature.

One of the principles of the Power of Opposite Strengths is that every person is naturally out of balance in each of the three pairs of opposite strengths. That is, every person naturally leads with one of the strengths in each pair. Identifying our lead strengths in each pair results in a particular combination of three lead strengths. This combination of three lead strengths is what determines one's natural pattern of strengths.

Some of us lead with thinking. Others of us lead with risking. These two strengths have equal value in human life, and which way a person happens to lean is neither good nor bad. The Power of Opposite Strengths says that if you have a lead strength in thinking—fine! Be an active thinker and use your risking as a supporting strength to make your thinking more productive and creative. If you have a lead strength in risking—fine! Actively risk and use your thinking as a supporting strength to make your risking more productive and creative. The Power of Opposite Strengths provides no basis on which to judge one strength as inherently more important and valuable than its opposite. It is true that one or the other may need to be emphasized at different times and in different situations, but we are talking about the need for an expression of a particular strength in a particular situation, not an evaluation of the intrinsic value of the strength itself.

If thinking is your lead strength, you are likely to be more stable than dynamic, more of a "head-person" than a "heart-person."

You like to reason things out and look before you leap. You are cautious and deliberate in your decision-making. You tend to be emotionally reserved and usually keep a tight rein on your feelings. You are probably better at organizing and planning than you are at putting the plan into action.

On the other hand, if risking is your lead strength, you are likely to feel and behave quite differently. You are a dynamic, moving kind of a person—more oriented toward action than thought. You readily take chances and leave yourself vulnerable. You get involved and express your feelings. You trust your feelings and aggressively seek interaction with other people. You tend to decide quickly and move into action without much delay.

If you lean more toward thinking, your decisions are likely to be based mostly on rational analysis. If you lean more the other way—toward the risking side—you tend to make your decisions more on intuitive feel. These two ways of making decisions are equally valuable. One way is not inherently better than the other is.

We feel most comfortable and are most effective when we lead with our naturally dominant strength. Those who have a lead strength in thinking naturally lead with rational analysis and use their intuitive feel as a supporting and energizing strength. Those who have a lead strength in risking naturally lead with their intuitive feel and use thinking as a supporting and stabilizing strength.

A person who leads in thinking tends to learn best when given an opportunity to think about it first and then get involved. That is simply not so with those who lead in risking. They learn best through immediate personal involvement. Thinkers tend to say, "Let me think about it first. Then I will be prepared to experience it." People who lead in risking do the opposite. They say, "Let me experience it first. Then I want to think about my experience and see what it means."

We observe this happening with those who attend our Opposite Strengths Seminars. Sometimes we furnish the participants with a book and ask them to read it before the seminar begins. During the seminar, we ask, "Who has read the book?" We find that almost all of those who lead in thinking have read the book, but hardly any of those who lead in risking have even bothered to open it. People who lead in risking want to experience the seminar first, and then read about it. People who lead in thinking want to read about it before they attend the seminar.

Two different approaches to life have been presented. These approaches are based upon the proposition that every person has a natural lead strength in either thinking or risking. Those who lead in thinking approach life mostly on an intellectual basis. For them, things have to make sense. They make their decisions primarily through rational analysis and learn best by thinking about things. On the other hand, those who lead in risking approach life mostly on a feeling basis. Things have to feel right. They make their decisions primarily on intuitive feel and learn most efficiently through experience—by actually doing it.

Thinking and risking are the two basic strengths that blend together in a creative life. They seem to be opposites in many ways, and sometimes we feel them pulling us in different directions. At times, the blending of those two strengths appears to be a paradox. How can a person be both stable and dynamic at the same time? How are we going to be emotionally involved and objective at the same time? What does it look like when we blend reason with emotion? How do these two strengths actually relate to each other?

The Power of Opposite Strengths answers these questions by saying that the two strengths relate as symbiotic, opposite strengths—each one feeding on the other's fruit and becoming creative in the process. We can say that we use our thinking strength to make our risking more creative and effective, and we use our risking strength to make our thinking more creative and productive.

The athletic equipment company Nike came up with a great slogan several years ago—"Just Do It." That slogan perfectly expresses what someone who leads in risking would believe. "Just Do It" means moving ahead without the full understanding that an equal emphasis on thinking would bring. We are just waiting for a company to come out with the opposite slogan of "Just Think It."

## The Thinking Pair— Practical Thinking/Theoretical Thinking

Now let's consider the two thinking strengths—practical thinking and theoretical thinking. These two thinking strengths are opposite to each other, and, when blended together, they produce our total reasoning, thinking abilities.

Every person has both kinds of thinking. We see how things are, and we see how things could be. We deal with facts, and we deal with ideas. We identify problems and see possible solutions. We live with reality and dream about a better tomorrow. Life would not be human without these two strengths.

Although we think in both ways all the time, one or the other is always in the foreground. Sometimes the emphasis is on practical problems: How am I going to get enough money to pay my bills? At other times, the emphasis is on our imagination: What a delight it would be to be lounging on Waikiki Beach! When one kind of thinking is in the foreground, the other recedes into the background, but the one in the background is still active, even if we are not conscious of it.

Both types of thinking are always active, and we constantly shift emphasis from one to the other. Sometimes situations demand that we shift, and at other times, we deliberately choose to shift. This ability to make the shift by personal choice is part of our basic freedom as human beings.

We all have both kinds of thinking ability, and we are continually shifting emphasis from one to the other. In addition, we are naturally better at one type of thinking than we are at the other. We are naturally out of balance in our thinking. Some people lean toward the practical, while others lean toward the theoretical.

Jay Thomas, the senior author, happens to favor the theoretical and has throughout his life. As a child, he tended to be a daydreamer, and it was a problem for him to shift his attention to the practical problem at hand. He preferred to read and live in his own thoughts. Even now, he delights in coming up with new ideas but finds it an effort to keep up with the practical things that he must do.

Every person naturally leans one way or the other—toward the practical or the theoretical. Which way we happen to lean says something important about our basic nature, but it says nothing about our value as a person. These two kinds of thinking have equal value in creative thinking, and by nature, we all are bound to lean one way or the other. This being the case, there is no good reason why we should look up to or down upon another person because of his or her tendency to favor one or the other of the two types of thinking.

In the early development of the Power of Opposite Strengths, the words "concrete" (for practical thinking) and "abstract" (for theoretical thinking) were used to identify the two types of thinking. The term "abstract" was problematic, however. Many people tended to associate it with abstract painting and therefore could not identify positively with that strength. In the early 1970s, the word "theoretical" was adopted instead and has served its purpose very well.

If you have a lead strength in practical thinking, you are likely to be realistic and down to earth. You probably prefer to deal with facts rather than ideas. You are more concerned with the problem at hand than you are the overall concept. You like to collect facts and see how things really work. You look for the practical way. Usually you are more skillful at applying an idea than you are at dealing with the idea itself. When you describe a situation, you prefer to use specifics rather than general terms.

If theoretical thinking is your lead strength, you tend to be philosophical and idealistic. You think more in terms of generalities than specifics. You look for the general principle. Frequently, you are imaginative. You tend to imagine possibilities and alternatives. You like to theorize and think about the overall concept. You enjoy talking about ideas and continually ask the question, "Why?"

Creative thinking is a blended interaction of these two types of thinking. It is a human manifestation of the Power of Opposite Strengths in which each strength generates its own unique product by feeding on products of its opposite. Practical thinking activity produces an awareness of the facts. These facts become the raw materials used by theoretical thinking to produce new concepts and ideas. In turn, the concepts produced by theoretical thinking become the tools used by practical thinking to produce an even greater awareness of the facts. In a creative person, this give and take interaction is continuous.

In his book *Good to Great*, Jim Collins coined the phrase the "Stockdale Paradox." Vice Admiral Jim Stockdale was the highest-ranking officer in captivity at the Hanoi Hilton during the Viet Nam war. Stockdale was able to survive through the mental model he created. He recognized and accepted the brutal facts of his existence, and he simultaneously had complete faith that he would eventually get out alive and become well again. Stockdale was exercising both practical and theoretical thinking, and being in that *process* created the fertile conditions that allowed his mind to endure his captivity.

# The Risking Pair—
# Dependent Risking/Independent Risking

Now we will consider the two risking strengths: dependent risking and independent risking. These two poles of risking have equal status, and, when blended together, they make our risking creative.

Again, as before, the impact of Paul Tillich's book *The Courage to Be* on Jay Thomas's original formulations should be acknowledged. In this instance, the book significantly helped to shape Jay's understanding of the nature of creative risking. Tillich identified two kinds of courage: the "courage to be oneself" and the "courage to be a part." Jay immediately saw a parallel with the Power of Opposite Strengths, which was taking form in his mind at that time. Tillich was describing two types of courage that were opposites, and each had a positive value.

For Jay, the most striking revelation was the idea that being dependent (Tillich's "courage to be a part") could be regarded as a strength. Like most people, Jay had been taught that being dependent was the sign of a weak person. The value system he had learned was one in which independence was the real strength and a quality to be admired. Its opposite—dependence—was something to be ashamed of and gotten rid of as you grew stronger. The concept that dependence could be regarded as a strength came as a shock to him.

Because a negative view of the word "dependence" seems to be a commonly held attitude in our society, Jay was very hesitant about using the term during the development of the Power of Opposite Strengths. For a long time, he used the term "courage to be in relationship" when talking about dependence. This worked fairly well and approached the meaning of dependence, but still did not go directly to the opposite meaning that he thought was needed. Finally, in the mid-70s, he decided to go with meaning over connotation and adopt the word "dependence" as the key descriptor for this strength. It began appearing in all Power of Opposite Strengths printed matter at that time, and it has been in use ever since. Happily, it has worked. Using the word "dependence" allows us to face the issue directly and describe the basic meaning of this strength more accurately.

Dependent risking is an others-oriented strength. It permits us to establish a relationship, to depend upon others, and to draw strength from them. Through this strength, we develop confidence in others and learn to trust them. We use this strength when we delegate to others. It also allows us to become a part of a community and receive emotional support and approval from other people. Through being dependent, we are encouraged by others and actually participate in their strength. Our dependent strength is our avenue to the world and all the values that wait for us out there. It is called a risking strength because we run a risk when we express it. When we lay ourselves open in an act of dependence, we become vulnerable. Our defenses are down, and we are at the mercy of the world. People can take advantage of us, and we can be hurt.

In contrast, independent risking is a self-oriented strength. It gives us the strength to depend upon ourselves and follow our own convictions. It lets us stand on our own two feet and make our own decisions. As we express independence, we develop self-confidence and become aware of ourselves. We know who we are. Through its expression, we experience personal freedom and create personal power. It gives us a sense of self-worth and significance. Just as with our dependent strength, we run a risk whenever we express our independent strength. When we separate ourselves out as distinct individuals, we run the risk of losing our relationships. We may lose the support and approval of others. We may find ourselves cut off from the community and be alone.

All of us have the courage to risk both dependence and independence. It is a natural part of being human. Both strengths are continuously active as we live our lives. However, we are continually shifting emphasis back and forth from one to the other. Sometimes we express our independence strongly, and our dependence recedes into the background. At other times, we emphasize our dependence by actively seeking the support and approval of others. When we do this, our independence recedes into the background.

Sometimes we make extreme shifts from one to the other. This dramatic shift from extreme independence to extreme dependence is characteristic of teen-agers. One minute they are extremely independent, and the next minute, they are extremely dependent. This is how they learn to express independence and dependence in a blended way. As they mature, the extreme shifts from one to the other are replaced by a blend of both strengths. As they develop a healthy and unique personality, their own natural inclination toward either independence or dependence continues to give a distinct flavor to their personality, but they also have greater flexibility and skill in shifting to their supporting strength when needed.

Not only do we shift emphasis from one type of courage to the other as the need arises, but we are naturally stronger in one than the other. One is easier for us to express than the other one is. Some people find it easier and more natural to express independence. Others find it easier and more comfortable to express dependence. Which way we happen to lean says something important about our natural way of being but says nothing about how much courage we have. It takes just as much courage to express dependence as it does to express independence. The only difference is that we risk losing different things when we express the two.

If you naturally lead in dependent risking, you are likely to enjoy working with a group. People know you for your cooperation and your willingness to consider the views of others. Relationships with others are very important to you. You find it easy to depend on others. You seek other people's opinions and rely on what they say. Their support and approval mean a great deal to you. You are people-oriented and you experience a great deal of warmth toward others. You are accepting, understanding and tolerant of others. You are supportive in your relationships.

If independence is your lead strength, you tend to feel quite a lot of self-confidence and self-sufficiency. You like to work on your own and tend to keep your own counsel. You are inclined to follow your own convictions and value your independence. You frequently feel competitive with others and tend to have quite a lot of ambition. It is easier for you to depend on yourself than to depend on others. You tend to be territorial.

Creative risking is a process that works in the same way as creative thinking. It is a blended interaction of the two types of risking in which each one feeds on the fruit of the other. Expressions of independence feed on the support and approval of others (the fruit of dependence). Said another way, the support of others encourages us to be more independent. Conversely, expressions of dependence feed on our self-confidence (the fruit of independence). In other words, we feel enough self-confidence to go ahead and risk dependence on others. We feel confident that even if they let us down, we can still stand on our own strengths.

In Stephen Covey's book *The 7 Habits of Highly Effective People*, he states that the process of growth is to proceed from dependence to independence to interdependence. The problem with this way of looking at how we relate to the world is that it treats dependence as subordinate to independence. As we see it, dependence and independence are equal but opposite strengths that work in tandem in a creative interaction that grows both of them. We do not believe that dependence is a stage one goes through en route to independence.

# Eight Patterns of Strengths

When the lead strength in each of the three pairs of opposite strengths is identified, the result is a particular combination of three lead strengths. This combination of three lead strengths determines the pattern of strengths. Since there are eight possible combinations of three lead strengths, there are eight natural patterns. Each one gives its own distinctive flavor to a particular personality.

Listed below are the eight possible combinations of three lead strengths. At the right of each is the pattern number that has arbitrarily been assigned to that combination:

| Three Lead Strengths | Pattern Number |
| --- | --- |
| Thinking/Practical/Dependent | I |
| Thinking/Practical/Independent | II |
| Thinking/Theoretical/Dependent | III |
| Thinking/Theoretical/Independent | IV |
| Risking/Dependent/Practical | V |
| Risking/Dependent/Theoretical | VI |
| Risking/Independent/Practical | VII |
| Risking/Independent/Theoretical | VIII |

# Patterns of Strengths

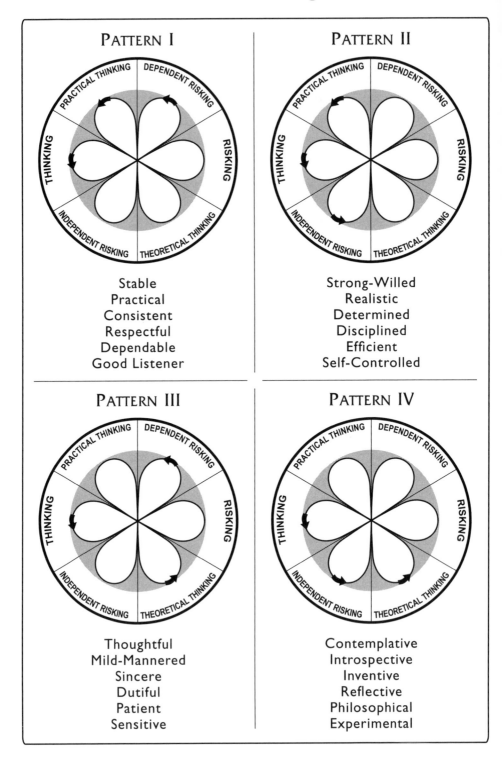

Figure 4a

# Patterns of Strengths

## PATTERN V

Outgoing
Friendly
Helpful
Caring
Adaptable
Sociable

## PATTERN VI

Diplomatic
Gracious
Soft-Hearted
Open
Warm
Trusting

## PATTERN VII

Self-Assertive
Action-Oriented
Enterprising
Self-Confident
Forceful
Takes Initiative

## PATTERN VIII

Dynamic
Persuasive
Imaginative
Innovative
Has Vision
Stimulates Change

*Figure 4b*

All eight patterns are displayed in Figure 4. Each pattern drawing is composed of three intersecting infinity symbols. The two basic strengths are at opposite ends of the horizontal infinity symbol, with thinking on the left and risking on the right. The two thinking strengths are at opposite ends of the infinity symbol that runs from upper left to lower right. Practical thinking is at the upper left, and theoretical thinking at the lower right. The two risking strengths are at opposite ends of the infinity symbol that runs from upper right to lower left, with dependent risking on the upper right and independent risking at the lower left.

An arrow appears at the end of the infinity symbol associated with the lead strength in each pair of strengths. This arrow identifies the strength with which a person who has this pattern naturally *begins*. It is the strength the person will tend to draw upon first in any given situation.

The infinity symbols are all drawn the same size to indicate that the pattern does not provide any information about the *amounts* of strengths a person has. The pattern simply *identifies* the lead and supporting strengths within each pair of opposite strengths.

Patterns, I, II, III, and IV all have a lead strength in thinking and a supporting strength in risking. This is represented by the arrow at the end of the thinking side of the basic pair's infinity symbol. On the other hand, Patterns V, VI, VII, and VIII have risking as the lead strength. This is depicted by the arrow at the end of the risking side of the basic pair infinity symbol.

Practical thinking is the lead strength in Patterns I, II, V, and VII. This is indicated by the arrow at the end of the practical thinking side of the thinking pair's infinity symbol. In Patterns III, IV, VI, and VIII, theoretical thinking is the lead strength. In these patterns, the arrow is at the end of the theoretical thinking side of the thinking pair's infinity symbol.

Since Patterns II, IV, VII, and VIII have a lead strength in independent risking, the arrow appears at the end of the independent risking side of the risking pair's infinity symbol. Patterns I, III, V, and VI have a lead strength in dependent risking. In these patterns, therefore, the arrow appears at the end of the dependent risking side of the risking pair's infinity symbol.

Our next task is to describe how each of these eight patterns of strengths is expressed in the life of a particular person. One of the principles of the Power of Opposite Strengths is that each pattern creates a constant force—a foundation—that produces distinctive personality characteristics. The rest of this section is devoted to describing the personality strengths and characteristics that tend to be produced by each pattern.

---

We wish to state as clearly, definitely, and emphatically as possible that the pattern of strengths is *not* a "personality type." Each individual has access to all six strengths and uses all six strengths in his or her daily life. The pattern simply indicates which strengths an individual will naturally turn to first in responding to various situations.

---

As a first step, we can divide the eight patterns into two groups of four. The first four patterns (Patterns I, II, III, and IV) tend to produce thinkers—intellectual, rational, reasoning people. On the other hand, the last four patterns (V, VI, VII, and VIII) tend to produce doers—dynamic, moving, action-oriented people. Since the lead strength is emphasized in the pattern description, the supporting strength is automatically de-emphasized. In that instance or at any other time that a descriptive word pointing to the lead strength is used, it is important to keep in mind that the supporting strength is also present and active. In other words, thinkers are also doers, and doers are also thinkers. It is simply a matter of which of the two is the lead strength.

As a second step, let's consider the eight patterns in pairs. Patterns I and II produce many similar personality characteristics. Both patterns lead in basic thinking and practical thinking. The combination of these two lead strengths tends to produce a rational, realistic, fact-oriented person. Those who have one of these two patterns of strengths tend to be practical people who see things as they are. They concentrate on the present and deal with the realities of a situation. They put things in order and bring stability to an organized effort. Patterns I and II tend to produce realistic people.

The next pair—Patterns III and IV—also has thinking as a lead strength. However, these patterns are different from Patterns I and II in that they have their dominant strength on the theoretical side. This combination tends to produce people who delight in dealing with ideas and concepts. They usually enjoy going to school and are naturally geared to doing well in scholastic pursuits. They like to gather knowledge and tend to have a philosophical bent. Patterns III and IV tend to produce idealistic people.

People who have the third pair—Patterns V and VI—have other people as their main focus in life. Those who have these patterns tend to be warm and outgoing people. They enjoy being with other people and thrive on recognition and compliments. Frequently, people who have these natural patterns are highly effective in sales—and particularly so in situations that require a soft sell. Patterns V and VI tend to produce people who are active, dynamic, and assertive in their efforts to establish warm and close relationships.

The last pair—Patterns VII and VIII—share quite a number of common personality characteristics. People who have these patterns of strengths are usually very much aware of their own strengths and have a clear idea of what they are trying to accomplish. They are goal-oriented. They usually feel a good deal of self-confidence and are self-assertive in their relationships. They are self-starters and experience a high drive to accomplish. Those who have Patterns VII and VIII are dynamic, enthusiastic, action-oriented people. They take the initiative and provide out-front leadership. They want to score.

Hopefully, nothing negative or depreciating has been said or implied about any of the patterns. That would not be consistent with the Power of Opposite Strengths, which holds that each pattern has its own unique blend of strengths to contribute to the creative process. Moreover, since we are dealing only with different patterns of equally valuable strengths, we have no basis on which to judge one pattern as superior to or more important than any other pattern. While particular kinds of strengths and patterns are needed to do the best job in particular situations, this has nothing to do with the intrinsic value of the patterns themselves. A person has every right to feel good about his or her own natural pattern of strengths, whatever it may be. In the value system of the Power of Opposite Strengths, all people are truly created equal (i.e., are equal in worth as individuals).

Now that we have considered the patterns in pairs, we will consider each one separately. In our earlier discussion, Patterns I and II were described as being very similar. Both lead in basic thinking, and both have their greatest strength in practical think-ing. Now let's look at how they are different. They differ in that Pattern I leads in dependent risking, and Pattern II leads in inde-pendent risking. This has an enormous impact on how people with these patterns tend to feel and behave.

When we are dealing with management people, we use the term "kindly administrator" to describe, in a general way, the characteristics of people who have Pattern I opposite strengths. In contrast, we use the term "control manager" when we talk about the style of management usually displayed by those who have Pattern II strengths. Those who have Pattern I strengths tend to run a family type of operation in which everyone is cared for as a person and there is an emphasis on human values. In contrast, those having Pattern II strengths tend to place more value on efficiency and productivity. They tend to pay more attention to production and less attention to the people involved. Those who have Pattern I strengths tend to run a loose ship, whereas those who have Pattern II strengths tend to run a tight ship. Either approach, loose or tight, can be creative, productive, and enjoyable, depending upon what the situation requires.

*Those who have Pattern I strengths are dependable and consistent.* They are conservative, accepting people and are usually good listeners. Their stability, warmth, and practicality make the world a comfortable place in which to live. An example quite close to home comes in the form of Jane Thomas, Jay's wife of almost 60 years. Jane has the Pattern I combination of strengths, and for several years did a masterful job of managing the administration of the Bi/Polar office. She calmly and effectively handled problems with our seminar leaders that would have driven Jay (who has Pattern IV strengths) to distraction. "When she got on the telephone," Jay is fond of saying, "things just seemed to settle down, and problems got solved. When we were married in 1947, I didn't know I was getting this added bonus."

Those who have Pattern I strengths tend to experience a persistent need for more self-confidence. We have interviewed hundreds of people who have this pattern, and we estimate that about 90 percent of them say they feel a need for more self-confidence. Although all of us feel a need for more self-confidence at times, those who have this pattern feel the need more deeply and more consistently. Another need they have is to think in more positive ways, particularly about themselves. They tend to underrate themselves, especially in groups. Because of this tendency to think negatively of themselves, they sometimes feel depressed.

*Those who have Pattern II strengths are realistic and independent.* They are usually reserved and private people. They initiate stability, while those who have Pattern I strengths tend to maintain it. People with Pattern II strengths are usually strong on self-discipline. They tend to feel self-sufficient and self-confident. They are stimulated by a tough challenge and derive a great deal of enjoyment out of personal accomplishment. "Efficiency" is their middle name.

People who have Pattern II strengths usually express a need for better communication with others. They tend to hold a tight rein on their feelings and not share them with other people. This interferes with their ability to communicate on a personal level. Another thing that interferes with their relationships is their tendency to think negatively of others. They are very good at spotting the shortcomings of other people—and they are usually right! This ability can be of great value. If it is left unchecked, however, it can certainly interfere with good relationships and openness in communication. Pattern IIs usually want to relate to others in a warmer and accepting way, but they have to consciously work at it.

The term "warm" is not used to describe the people who have Pattern II strengths. However, this does not mean that people with this pattern can't be warm people. They can be genuinely warm toward others as they grow in maturity and learn to express their relationship strengths in their own way. A company president with whom Jay Thomas worked from 1973 to 1985 is an outstanding example of this fact. He has clear Pattern II strengths. He is aware of this and affirms it along with almost everyone else who knows him well. He is also an extremely warm person, as others in the company acknowledge based on their own personal relationships with him. Thus, while his Pattern II strengths show through clearly, he is still a very warm person who genuinely cares for others. The maturity toward which this points was manifested in his exceptional effectiveness as the CEO of his company. Under his leadership, it became a very people-oriented company. It also increased its profits tenfold during the time Jay worked with him.

Now we will turn our attention to those people who have natural patterns III and IV. People who have these patterns are similar in that they are thinkers and are stronger on the theoretical side. They are different in that those with Pattern III strengths lean toward dependent risking, and those with Pattern IV strengths lean toward independence. This disparity in risking orientation makes a big difference in how these people feel and behave. It also makes a difference in what they can do the best.

*Those who have Pattern III strengths are idealistic and cooperative.* They have a natural ability to understand other people's ideas and concepts. They usually have a good ability to understand proven theories and relate them to one another. Beyond this, they are usually effective in communicating these concepts to other people. Their people-centeredness frequently expresses itself in student-centered teaching. Those who have this pattern frequently find teaching to be an appropriate vocation.

All of those with Pattern III or IV strengths tend to be technical people, but Pattern IIIs and Pattern IVs express their technical abilities in very different ways. Frequently, people who have Pattern III strengths are very effective in heading up research and development operations. They tend to be thorough, careful, academic, and oriented toward research. They usually have a good ability to compare one theory to another. On the other hand, those who have Pattern IV strengths usually express their technical ability through intuitive insights in the development of new ideas. Where people with Pattern III strengths usually prefer to work as members of a group, those with Pattern IV strengths usually prefer to work alone.

People who have Pattern III strengths tend to feel a persistent need for more self-confidence. In this way, they are very similar to those with Pattern I strengths. They are forever selling themselves short and underrating their own importance. They tend to think about themselves in this way: "What I have to say doesn't amount to much, so I will just keep quiet and not say anything." Almost always, those having this pattern feel a painful need to develop more self-confidence.

One of Jay Thomas's friends, a retired professor of Education at Perkins School of Theology at Southern Methodist University, has the Pattern III combination of strengths. He has all of the right credentials, including a Phi Beta Kappa and a Ph.D. from a respected eastern university. Jay first became acquainted with him in 1970 when the Power of Opposite Strengths was introduced to the faculty at Perkins. Through all the years since, he has consistently displayed the characteristics of people who have Pattern III strengths. He is philosophical, articulate, scholarly, cultured, thin-skinned, gentle, considerate, dutiful, and terribly conscientious. Not only does he show these strengths clearly, but he also affirms the needs that people with this pattern usually experience. He tends to think negatively of himself and experiences a painful need to be more assertive in his relationships. Although Jay has observed a great deal of growth in him during their acquaintanceship, his friend reports that his point of pain is still in that same place.

*Those who have Pattern IV strengths are inventive and self-confident.* They react differently than those who have Pattern III strengths. Rather than read about other people's theories, they have a strong inclination to develop their own ideas. People who have Pattern IV strengths stay more within themselves, while those with Pattern III strengths tend to reach out more to other people.

People with Pattern IV strengths have leaps of insight that are sometimes brand new. This frequently causes a problem. Although an intuitive insight may be accurate, it may also take a long time to fill in the gap between where other people are and the point to which the Pattern IV has leaped.

To compound the problem, Pattern IVs have great difficulty in documenting how they arrived at their intuitive insight. They don't arrive at their insights in a systematic, linear thinking process. They do it with a quantum leap, and then they have to go back and fill in the logical steps. This is not to say that their intuitive insights are always right. Their insights are usually in the ballpark, however. If their intuitive insights are shaped and sharpened by reality, they frequently evolve into very useful ideas.

The Pattern IV combination is Jay Thomas's own natural pattern, and he has experienced all the strengths and the problems that go with it. He delights in dealing with ideas and particularly enjoys coming up with a new insight. He also thoroughly enjoys philosophy and thinking about abstract ideas. "It is well nigh impossible for me to describe the great feeling I have when a new idea comes to me," he has said. "To me, the experience of having a new idea is the closest I ever come to complete happiness. When it happens, I have a strong sense of well-being. I really feel good."

Jay gives what he considers to be a classic example. In 1973, he was working with two faculty members at Southern Methodist University on a new revision for the Bi/Polar seminar workbook. One night, en route to a meeting with them on the campus, Jay had an enormous insight concerning how two opposite strengths relate to each other. It was already clear to him that the two strengths in an opposite pair were both positive, and that both became stronger in the growth process. What he had not understood up to that point was how they related to each other in order to bring that about. "Before the insight came," he reports,

## Jay Thomas on the Everyday Problems of Those Who Have Pattern IV Strengths

Becoming aware of the problems that are normal for people with Pattern IV strengths has helped me deal with my own problems. People with my pattern typically have difficulty communicating their intuitive insights. Usually, they emphasize the theory and fail to communicate on a practical level. This has been a frustrating problem for me, particularly in the early days when the Power of Opposite Strengths was taking form. In those days, when I conducted seminars, I was sure of my insights, but about all I would do was to continually repeat the concepts in abstract terms. This resulted in rather dry and boring theoretical lectures that were highly ineffective. I needed to make my thinking creative by taking a dose of my own medicine.

Recognizing that it was my problem helped me start looking for a solution. The solution was simple: I needed to communicate the concepts by giving examples. I found I was much less frustrated and communicated much more effectively when I shifted to the practical and gave examples, rather than just repeating the concept in another abstract form.

I have always had a problem in understanding what is going on between me and another person emotionally. I recognize that I have a tendency to be somewhat reserved and standoffish. It is very difficult for me to express my dependence on others. Even to admit I am dependent on others has been a chore for me. The Power of Opposite Strengths has helped me realize that dependence is really a strength. This realization has enabled me to admit and express my dependent feelings more fully. In turn, it has made me a warmer person in my relationships. Now I enjoy people much more and get a real emotional lift from my relationships. This is a new and delightful experience for me. I believe this positive emotional support from others has enabled me to express my natural strengths even more strongly.

"I was not at all clear about what I was looking for. The best I can describe it is to say that I was uneasy. I felt confused and unsure. I was agitated and worried. Just before the insight came, I felt a good deal of depression. The whole Power of Opposite

Strengths just seemed to fall apart at my feet. Then, all of a sudden, the insight came. It was very simple: Opposite strengths feed each other! With it came a tremendously good feeling. It was a mountaintop experience for me."

To this day Jay can remember precisely where he was when it happened—about 100 yards from the Mockingbird Lane exit on Central Expressway, going toward downtown Dallas. He floated on over to the meeting eager to share his insight with his colleagues. After a few minutes of work on the new workbook, Jay was unable to contain himself any longer. He blurted out his idea and demonstrated it with the infinity symbol that is displayed in Figure 1. He traced the figure, showing how he conceived of each of the strengths producing a fruit that fed the other. His colleagues nodded their heads, said, "Uh huh," and started talking about something else. Although Jay was disappointed that they did not share his excitement, his own enthusiasm and confidence in the insight was not dampened in the least. In fact, that reaction is typical for people who have Pattern IV strengths. What others think of their ideas is not nearly as important to them as their own mental clarity and internal conviction.

People who have Pattern IV strengths experience many of the same needs as those with Pattern II strengths, especially in their relationships. One of their most painful needs is for better communication with others, particularly on an emotional level. Those who have natural pattern IV frequently feel uncomfortable in social situations. They usually want to talk about ideas (especially their own) and are frustrated with small talk. They hardly know what to say in a light conversation. It takes quite a lot of learning for them just to enjoy other people. They tend to view a relationship with someone else as a means to an end—not an as end in itself.

Now it is time to look at people who have Patterns V and VI as their natural combination of lead strengths. They are the warm people of the world. This is not to say that those of us who have other natural patterns are *not* warm, but it is to say that people who have Patterns V and VI place a premium on warm relationships with others and have a natural talent for developing them. People who have these two patterns are similar in that they all tend to be outgoing and take the initiative in establishing a relationship. Both are usually effective in soft-sell situations. They are different in that the people who have Pattern V strengths lean toward practicality, while those who have Pattern VI strengths tend to be more romantic and lean toward idealism.

Although all of us want and need recognition from others, it is especially important to the people who have these two patterns. They almost demand to be told how you feel about them. Again, we all like praise. For those who have Pattern V and VI strengths, however, praise, and compliments can't come too often.

They are very social people and usually have highly developed social skills. They feel comfortable with others. They are very accepting and sympathetic, and they enjoy relationships for their own sake. In social situations, others frequently find themselves following along in their warm wake.

*Those having Pattern V strengths are outgoing and practical.* They are usually effective in jobs requiring skill in coordinating the activities of others. They are very aware of what is going on inside people and are especially sensitive to their feelings. This base of awareness gives them a great deal of skill in communication, particularly on an emotional level. They know how others are feeling and what it takes to please them. Frequently, they are good counselors. They feel comfortable dealing with feelings and are usually effective in getting others to share their feelings with them. The practicality inborn in those with Pattern V strengths is frequently used to help others find practical solutions to their relationship problems.

In business, many of those who have Pattern V strengths go into personnel work, which gives them many opportunities to help people in practical ways. A job in training and development seems to fit their natural strengths very well, and it usually makes them effective as training specialists.

*People who have Pattern VI strengths are assertive and intuitive about people.* They are emotionally expressive and frequently have a flair for dramatics. A number of professional entertainers have the Pattern VI combination of strengths. One of their great strengths is an intuitive feel for an audience. Because of this, they have a powerful ability to move their audiences emotionally.

Many of those who have Pattern VI strengths find that the public relations business fits their natural talents very well. They usually have a good facility with words and ideas, and they enjoy being involved with lots of people.

Jay Thomas's account of some coaching he did recently with a public relations man is instructive. Jay found the gentleman to be warm, talkative, outgoing, and witty, and he was very comfortable in his presence. Sure enough, the *Opposite Strengths Inventories* showed that the client had Pattern VI strengths. The problem the man was experiencing was not difficult to uncover, either. For the past nine years, he had been working for a man who constantly belittled him, thus robbing him of his self-confidence. He was in the right field, but he was working for the wrong man. He changed jobs and went to another public relations firm. If his new employer recognizes his talents and encourages him, he should be quite successful in his new job.

People who have Pattern V and VI strengths experience very similar needs. One of their most frequent pains is that they let the demands of others rule their lives. Many of them also say that their greatest need is for more self-confidence. Most of them wish they could be more self-assertive and stand up for their own rights more effectively.

Now we will consider Pattern VII and VIII individually. We often refer to those who have Patterns V and VI strengths as "soft-sell people." In contrast, those having natural patterns VII and VIII are "hard-sell people." They take an independent stance and strongly assert their own views and opinions. People who have these two patterns are similar in that they are both independent riskers and have a good deal of self-confidence. They are different in that those having Pattern VII strengths lean toward facts and reality, where those with Pattern VIII strengths lean toward ideas and visions of the possibilities.

*People who have Pattern VII strengths are self-assertive and enterprising.* They are clearly the Horatio Alger, pull-yourself-up-by-the-bootstraps kind of people. This pattern represents the strength of our American hero—the true pioneer, the practical, self-reliant, enterprising hero of the American dream. They are characterized by Yankee practicality and feet-on-the-ground realism. They feel comfortable being out-front leaders. They want other people to interact with them and follow their leadership. Those with Pattern VII strengths are also high-drive people who have an intense desire to accomplish. They usually feel a great deal of self-confidence and willingly take calculated risks.

Pattern VIIs have an inborn intuitive feel for people and situations. They tend to fly by the seat of their pants. They are very competitive and are stimulated by a tough challenge. One of our friends who has Pattern VII strengths put it this way: "I don't like to lose worth a damn!"

People with Pattern VII strengths frequently start their own businesses from scratch. Their energy and willingness to take risks tend to make them hard-driving and successful salespeople. The companies they head up are usually aggressive, dynamic, and exciting, and they typically grow and expand rapidly. Mature Pattern VIIs recognize their own tendencies toward dynamism and change. As a result, they often end up bringing in someone with strong stabilizing strengths (usually a person with Pattern II strengths) to give balance to the organization. While a person with Pattern VII strengths is usually the president during a company's beginning and rapid growth period, it is typical for a person with the Pattern II combination of strengths to become the president of a large, already well-established company.

Of course, a person with *any* of the eight patterns, through maturity and self-discipline, can function effectively as president of a business. However, the strengths that are usually required to function effectively as a CEO in a business enterprise seem to match the natural lead strengths of those who have Pattern VII and Pattern II strengths more closely than the lead strengths of any of the other natural patterns.

In the early days of giving seminars, we used the label "promoter" to describe a person that has Pattern VIII strengths. Although the term still seems both descriptive and valid, it proved to be somewhat problematic. Sometime around 1973, Jay Thomas was conducting a seminar for a group of Methodist executives in the Dallas area, three of whom had Pattern VIII opposite strengths. He used "promoter" as a basic term to describe people who have this pattern. After Jay's presentation, one of the participants came up to him and said, somewhat facetiously, "Say, Doc, would it be all right with you if we call people with Pattern VIII strengths 'pioneers' rather than 'promoters'?" He was reacting to the con-man connotation in the term "promoter." Sympathetic with his comment, Jay stopped using the term in his presentations and replaced it with "pioneer." After a year or so, however, Jay found that "pioneer" just did not have the flavor and accuracy of "promoter." He took "promoter" out of retirement and still frequently uses it as a label for those having this pattern. Because the word is so descriptive of Pattern VIII, the risk of giving offense to people for whom it connotes hucksterism seems justified. He is also careful to emphasize that the pattern is composed only of strengths, and he explicitly warns everyone away from attaching any negative meanings the term.

*Those who have natural pattern VIII strengths are dynamic and persuasive.* They are people of vision who take the risks required to make their visions become real. People with Pattern VIII see the potential and have the courage to bet on what they see. They have the ability, through independence and imagination, to put promotional deals together. They get things going. They push, initiate, and sell a dream. They cause people to get excited and emotionally involved by seeing the potential. They are dynamic, personable, strong-impact people. In fact, people with natural pattern VIII tend to be the most dynamic people of all.

An instructive case study of Pattern VIII strengths arises from Jay's experiences when he was retained as a psychological consultant by a small college. When the president of the college (who had Pattern VIII strengths) had taken over the position about a year before, he had found an institution that was in crisis. The former president had resigned, the faculty was in a state of confusion and uncertainty, the college was in desperate need of financial support, and the board was giving serious thought to closing the school. It needed strong leadership if it were to survive. As it happened, the board had made a wise decision. They had hired a person with Pattern VIII strengths—a strong promoter—as president. Then they gave him free rein to exert his dynamic and inspiring leadership. By the time Jay arrived on the scene, the new president had already made considerable progress in turning gloom into hope. The administrative staff and faculty were beginning to share the president's confidence. They were starting to see and share his vision of what the college could become. The president was clearly the central force that turned the bankrupt college into what it is today: a dynamic institution that has hope for the future. He did many things to bring this about, and there were many people who joined his team in a common effort to do the job. He went for broke, and he won!

What are the points of pain for those who have Patterns VII and VIII? One of the problems most of them clearly recognize is a tendency to talk too much and not listen enough. Another common problem they share is impatience. Sometimes this impatience is expressed by pushing others to make quick decisions. They frequently get themselves into trouble by jumping to conclusions and moving too fast—deciding before they have had time to make a good judgment.

Another problem shared by people with Patterns VII and VIII is that they prefer to do things themselves. They find it difficult to step back and rely on other people. Many of them in business settings find that the most difficult thing they have to learn is delegating to another person—letting go and effectively getting the other person to assume responsibility.

People who have Patterns VII and VIII tend to experience different needs in their thinking. Those who have Pattern VII strengths tend to feel a need for a better grasp of abstract concepts. Those with Pattern VIII strengths feel a need for a better grasp of reality.

It would probably enhance understanding of the eight natural patterns if well-known personalities could be identified with each one. For example, although it will necessarily be a guessing game in the absence of systematic information, it may be instructive to associate a President of the United States with each of the eight patterns. Of course, there is no way we can say that they actually have particular patterns, but we certainly can note that they tend to show the personality characteristics normally produced by that pattern.

Dwight D. Eisenhower is a good choice to be a representative for Pattern I. The kinds of strengths he showed as Commander-in-Chief for the Allied Forces during World War II strongly suggest that he had the strengths of a Pattern I. He was skilled at organization, fostering stability, planning, and coordinating diverse groups, and he was know for sound and realistic thinking and warm and understanding leadership. Later, when he was President, people respected his conservative, stable leadership and expressed their warmth toward him with the endearing nickname "Ike."

Although he also expressed many of the characteristics of people who have Pattern VII strengths, Harry S. Truman seems to fit Pattern II. One of the reasons that Pattern II strengths fit is that he read extensively. His autobiography indicated that he read all the books in the Independence, Kansas library before he had finished high school. This indicates that he leaned more toward thinking than action. Many of his qualities—his objectivity, ability to make hard decisions independently, toughness, reality-orientation, and ability to cut through to the core of a problem point toward Truman having had Pattern II strengths.

Woodrow Wilson's natural strengths seem to fit Pattern III. His university background before he became President is also suggestive of this pattern. His idealism, as manifested by his involvement in the League of Nations, also points toward the Pattern III combination of strengths.

The independence, idealism, and ability to deal skillfully with concepts and words exhibited by Jack Kennedy point toward the strengths of a Pattern IV. Such historical figures as Leonardo DaVinci, Thoreau, Charles Darwin, Copernicus, and Albert Einstein also display the major characteristics produced by the Pattern IV blend of opposite strengths.

Jimmy Carter shows many of the characteristics of people who have Pattern V strengths. He appears to communicate extremely well, particularly on an emotional level. He displays a good deal of warmth and seems to live mostly in a world of people. He is also a very practical politician.

One of our seminar facilitators made a study of "Teddy" Roosevelt and concluded that he was a Pattern VI. His gregariousness and love of the natural environment are good clues that he was a Pattern VI. Will Rogers and Mark Twain are also excellent examples of Pattern VI.

We have many good examples of well-known people who showed Pattern VII characteristics. Lyndon B. Johnson fits Pattern VII very well. His style of leadership, particularly when he was a major figure in Congress, points clearly toward Pattern VII. Other examples are General George Patton (almost a textbook example), Charles DeGaulle, and Amelia Earhart.

Franklin D. Roosevelt appears to fit Pattern VIII. His persuasiveness and idealism suggest this pattern. His energy, self-confidence, vision of the New Deal, and fireside chats all point toward the characteristics of those who have Pattern VIII strengths. Others who appear to have had Pattern VIII strengths are Martin Luther King, Jr. ("I have a dream.") and Saint Paul.

# Identifying Your Own Natural Pattern

Your pattern of strengths is identified by discovering your lead strength in each of the three pairs of opposite strengths. This natural pattern determines your natural way of being and suggests how you can make your greatest contribution to the creative process.

Although you have a natural pattern of strengths that flavors everything you do, you also have the ability to emphasize any of your supporting strengths and express any of the eight patterns. Your ability to emphasize any of your strengths gives you the flexibility to respond differently to different situations and thus to adapt effectively to your environment. Being flexible in expressing your strengths is an essential part of being a creative and effective human being.

Your natural flexibility in expressing your strengths tends to mask your natural pattern, at least to the outside world. If you have developed a good deal of flexibility in expressing your supporting strengths, it will probably be more difficult for you to identify your natural pattern. This does not mean that you don't have a natural pattern. It just means that you will need to spend more time and effort in discovering what it is.

Most of us have been taught a value system that places more value on some core strengths than on others. If you have been taught a value system in which one of your lead strengths is depreciated, it will tend to cause you to block that strength and not show it to the outside world. It can influence you to hide your natural way and even make you want to be something other than what you really are at the core. Having a value system that depreciates one of your natural lead strengths can make it hard for you to accept and affirm your natural pattern.

Sometimes the demands of our environment have required that we exercise our supporting strengths so much that our lead strengths have been neglected. For example, your work situation may have required that you consistently exercise one of your supporting strengths. As a result, you may not have had the opportunity to experience fully and develop skill in expressing your natural lead strength. Consistently emphasizing one of your supporting strengths over a long period will not make it into a natural lead strength for you, but it may make it more difficult for you to identify your natural pattern.

One way to discover your natural pattern is to "try on" each of the eight patterns and see how it fits. You can do this by reading a description of the personality characteristics that each pattern tends to produce. (These descriptions appear at the end of this chapter.) The description that feels most natural or comfortable is an indicator of your natural pattern. Your self-perception, however, is subject to a number of distortions, such as seeing yourself as you would like to be instead of as you actually are, seeing yourself in limited situations, and paying attention to your learned behaviors instead of your natural pattern of strengths. That is why we developed our Other-report *Opposite Strengths Inventories*—so that we could capture the perceptions other people have about you in addition to your self-perceptions. Using information from both sources is the way to get the most accurate picture of who you really are. Any of our Opposite Strengths Certified Executive Coaches can give you access to the *Opposite Strengths Inventories* and coach you in using the results to bring Opposite Strengths principles into your life and relationships.

When they are trying to identify their lead strengths in each of the three pairs of strengths, most people find they are confident about their lead strength in one or two of the pairs. Their lead strength in the third pair is frequently less obvious and is sometimes very difficult for them to identify. This usually means they see themselves in two patterns and cannot decide which of the two is actually their natural pattern. Since these patterns have two lead strengths in common, they are closely related and produce many similar personality characteristics.

Each of the eight patterns has two lead strengths in common with three other patterns. These three closely related patterns are referred to as "flex-patterns." You will usually find that you display many of the characteristics described in your three flex-patterns. You can express each of your flex-patterns by emphasizing one of your supporting strengths. You may find that you can express one of your three flex-patterns rather easily and effectively but find it somewhat more difficult to express the other two. You may also find that expressing one of your flex-patterns is especially difficult. The three flex-patterns for each natural pattern are identified in the descriptions of the eight patterns found at the end of this chapter.

Each pattern also has an *opposite* pattern—the pattern that has opposite lead strengths in all three pairs. Here are the four combinations of opposite patterns:

- I and VIII
- II and VI
- III and VII
- IV and V.

You may be able to confirm the selection of your natural pattern by reading the description of your opposite pattern and feeling that it does not fit you at all.

Although you may be able to identify your own natural pattern by thinking subjectively about yourself within the context of the Power of Opposite Strengths, a more scientific and reliable way to identify your pattern is through the *Opposite Strengths Inventory*. This professionally validated psychological instrument is designed to reveal a person's natural pattern of strengths. As mentioned above, because your self-perception is subject to a number of distortions, the way to get the most accurate picture of who you really are is to use our Self-report and Other-report *Opposite Strength Inventories* in combination with each other.

Our *Inventories* are used in many different applications including corporate seminars and executive coaching experiences. More information on the history and technical aspects of the *Inventories* is presented in the section below.

# The *Opposite Strengths Inventories*

Development of the *Opposite Strengths Inventories* began with the birth of the Power of Opposite Strengths in the early 1960s. From the very beginning, some type of paper-and-pencil inventory has been used to help people discover their personal leanings in the three pairs of opposite strengths. Through the years, many different words and phrases have been used to describe the strengths, and a variety of inventory designs have been tried.

The *Inventories* now in use are the products of years of experience and extensive research that has been conducted since 1962. In 1977, Drs. Jay Thomas and Clyde Mayo (an industrial psychologist in Houston, Texas) jointly published a manual that gives a complete description of the *Inventory* and the research that made it a professionally validated instrument.

In 1982, Dr. Jay Thomas performed additional research that had a larger sample and used more sophisticated statistical techniques. The results of his study confirmed the original validity and reliability measurements obtained by Mayo and provided empirical information that has allowed us to make the instrument even more effective. Since that time, many other research studies using our *Analysis of Strengths* (the professional report used by our Certified Executive Coaches and Certified Facilitators in their work with other people) have been completed, and more are in progress. (You can learn more about our research through our Web site.)

Since the late 1960s, we have recommended that sets of six *Opposite Strengths Inventories* be used in order to obtain the best possible measurement of peoples' natural strengths. One *Inventory* is a Self-report completed out by the person himself or herself, and the other five are Other-reports filled out by other people who know him or her well. Originally, of course, everything was paper-based. All six of the *Inventories* in a set were mailed directly to our offices for computer processing. The final result was a two-page numerical *Analysis of Strengths* that was then disseminated to the individual through our Certified Executive Coaches and Certified Facilitators.

We have definitely changed with the times, and paper versions of the *Inventories* are no longer available. Instead, all *Inventories* are now being completed online at our Web site. Also, instead of six *Inventories*, you can now use an unlimited number of Opposite Strengths Inventories. Finally, in addition to the traditional numerical *Analysis of Strengths*, you may obtain our three online Guides – the *Guide to Being Yourself, Guide to Being Flexible*, and *Relationship Guide* – through your Member Home Page on our Web site. Note that to obtain the Opposite Strengths Inventories and the professional reports based on them, you must be receiving executive coaching from an Opposite Strengths Certified Executive Coach or attending an Opposite Strengths Seminar being conducted by an Opposite Strengths Certified Facilitator. For a complete, up-to-date description, please visit *www.oppositestrengths.com*.

Use of a self-report in combination with multiple other-reports is one of the unusual features of our measurement system. Indeed, the *Opposite Strengths Inventories* are pioneers among what are now known as "360 Degree Feedback" instruments. (We have been using them since the 1960s.) Obtaining information about both the person's self-image and how others see the person is extremely valuable in a number of ways.

First, it provides a wider database for the conclusions. The combined result that incorporates information from both Self- and Other-reports is more accurate than a result based on either perspective alone.

Second, the results tend to be more convincing. Frequently, a person's self-image agrees very closely with the view of others. When this happens, it invariably gives the person an added measure of confidence about accurate identification of his or her pattern.

Third, it is simply very interesting to most people to see how others view them. In addition, the insights they get from these *Inventories* can be used to great benefit to strengthen and deepen their relationships with other people.

Fourth, two people who have completed *Opposite Strengths Inventories* on our Web site can produce a *Relationship Guide* that pertains to the two of them. The *Relationship Guide* gives specific, detailed information to both people on the dynamics of their relationship and how to strengthen it.

The *Opposite Strengths Inventories* are now being used in many different applications. Complete information on how they are used and how they can make your own life and relationships more satisfying is available on our Web site. Whether you are interested in Opposite Strengths Seminars for your organization, to leverage your professional executive coaching practice for more income and impact, or in research, we welcome and encourage your continued relationship with us. If you have novel ideas on how the *Inventories* can be used, we would like to hear about those, too.

For more information on how to contact us, visit our Web site at *www.oppositestrengths.com.*

The following illustrations are from our Sustaining Your Success *Pocket Guide,* which can be purchased from our Web site.

# The Eight Patterns of Strengths

# Pattern I

| Lead Strengths | Thinking | Practical Thinking | Dependent Risking |
|---|---|---|---|
| **Supporting Strengths** | Risking | Theoretical Thinking | Independent Risking |
| **Flex-patterns** | V | III | II |
| **Personality Characteristics** | Stable, dependable, steady, orderly, quiet, consistent, methodical, cautious, receptive, hesitant, accepting, respectful, conforming, attentive, economical, practical, systematic, loyal. **Good listener – maintains stability.** | | |
| **Relationship Behaviors** | Focus of attention on the practical situation. Makes others feel secure and comfortable. Waits for other person to make the first move. Follows the leadership of others. Avoids confrontation and conflict. Keeps thoughts and feelings to self. | | |
| **Vocational Talents** | Maintains established routines. Watches over details. Provides a warm and accepting work environment. Keeps things running smoothly. Loyal and dependable team player. | | |
| **Wants Others To...** | Take the initiative in a respectful way. Ask for their help. Give them encouragement. Show them appreciation. Invite them to go along. | | |

*Figure 5a*

# Pattern II

| | | Practical<br>Thinking | Independent<br>Risking |
|---|---|---|---|
| **Lead Strengths** | Thinking | | |
| **Supporting Strengths** | Risking | Theoretical<br>Thinking | Dependent<br>Risking |
| **Flex-patterns** | VII | IV | I |
| **Personality Characteristics** | Rational, logical, analytical, objective, firm, deliberate, self-reliant, strong-willed, calm, conservative, industrious, self-controlled, determined, prudent, discerning, realistic, tenacious, disciplined.<br>**Objective thinker – uses common sense.** | | |
| **Relationship Behaviors** | Focus of attention on objective reality.<br>Provides stable leadership.<br>Brings rationality to emotional situations.<br>Keeps own counsel.<br>Holds feelings inside.<br>Avoids "small talk." | | |
| **Vocational Talents** | Analyzes problems.<br>Takes initiative to solve problems.<br>Brings order out of chaos.<br>Brings efficiency to operations.<br>Keeps tight control. | | |
| **Wants Others To...** | Listen to them.<br>Show them respect.<br>Give them space – don't crowd.<br>Stay rational and objective.<br>Give them the facts – preferably in writing. | | |

*Figure 5b*

# Pattern III

| Lead Strengths | Thinking | Theoretical Thinking | Dependent Risking |
|---|---|---|---|
| **Supporting Strengths** | Risking | Practical Thinking | Independent Risking |
| **Flex-patterns** | VI | I | IV |
| **Personality Characteristics** | Thoughtful, polite, sincere, knowledgeable, learned, academic, scholarly, sensitive, shy, mild-mannered, gentle, faithful, dutiful, patient, tolerant, benevolent, studious, courteous. **Fundamental philosopher— synthesizes information.** | | |
| **Relationship Behaviors** | Focus of attention on the relationship. Gives support in a quiet way. Careful not to hurt feelings. Understanding and affirming. Seeks to be cooperative and agreeable. Goes along with the group. | | |
| **Vocational Talents** | Organizes and communicates knowledge. Writes textbooks and historical works. Teaches and nurtures. Keeps cultural values alive. Advises in a sensitive and supportive way. | | |
| **Wants Others To...** | Take the initiative in a quiet way. Give them a chance to respond. Listen to their thoughts and ideas. Take the lead in making decisions. Include them in the action. | | |

*Figure 5c*

# Pattern IV

| Lead Strengths | Thinking | Theoretical Thinking | Independent Risking |
|---|---|---|---|
| **Supporting Strengths** | Risking | Practical Thinking | Dependent Risking |
| **Flex-patterns** | VIII | II | III |
| **Personality Characteristics** | Contemplative, reflective, introspective, philosophical, insightful, precise, accurate, experimental, serious, intense, persistent, self-sufficient, profound, earnest, inventive, individualistic, perceptive, ingenious. **Intuitive thinker—concentrates on one thing at a time.** | | |
| **Relationship Behaviors** | Focus of attention on own thoughts. Follows ideas rather than people. Works out problems alone. Reserved and private. Selective in choosing friendships. Reticent in social situations. | | |
| **Vocational Talents** | Has original ideas. Creates new products. Takes initiative to explore and invent. Catalyst for change. "Cut and try" inventor. | | |
| **Wants Others To...** | Be thoughtful and reserved. Ask for their thoughts and ideas. Give them time to think. Respect their privacy. Let them make their own decisions. | | |

*Figure 5d*

# Pattern V

| Lead Strengths | Risking | Practical Thinking | Dependent Risking |
|---|---|---|---|
| **Supporting Strengths** | Thinking | Theoretical Thinking | Independent Risking |
| **Flex-patterns** | I | VI | VII |
| **Personality Characteristics** | Outgoing, friendly, sociable, cordial, caring, talkative, generous, adaptable, supportive, giving, helpful, inclusive, gregarious, likeable, cooperative, accommodating, big-hearted, sympathetic. **Helpful coordinator—facilitates communication.** | | |
| **Relationship Behaviors** | Focus of attention on other person. Seeks to please others. Wants to interact and be involved. Gets feelings out on the table. Draws people into relationships. Avoids making enemies. | | |
| **Vocational Talents** | Coordinates practical projects. Works in "helping" professions. Does personnel work. Counsels in a warm way. Is a "soft-sell" salesperson. | | |
| **Wants Others To...** | Give recognition – every day. Show warm appreciation. Accept their help with gratitude. Trust them. Let them "talk out" problems. | | |

*Figure 5e*

# Pattern VI

| Lead Strengths | Risking | Theoretical Thinking | Dependent Risking |
|---|---|---|---|
| **Supporting Strengths** | Thinking | Practical Thinking | Independent Risking |
| **Flex-patterns** | III | V | VIII |
| **Personality Characteristics** | Diplomatic, gracious, hospitable, trusting, open, responsive, compassionate, liberal, empathetic, hopeful, humorous, cheerful, softhearted, demonstrative, idealistic, artful, affectionate, expressive. **Sensitive relator—gives to others.** | | |
| **Relationship Behaviors** | Focus of attention on relationships. Trusts others. Shows feelings openly. Seeks "closeness" and "intimacy." Makes others feel warm and accepted. Leaves self unprotected and exposed. | | |
| **Vocational Talents** | Entertains people. Works in public relations. Active in volunteer organizations. Diplomat. Performer. | | |
| **Wants Others To...** | Be receptive. Show warmth and compassion. Share feelings. Help them feel good about themselves. Give them compliments. | | |

*Figure 5f*

# Pattern VII

| Lead Strengths | Risking | Practical Thinking | Independent Risking |
|---|---|---|---|
| **Supporting Strengths** | Thinking | Theoretical Thinking | Dependent Risking |
| **Flex-patterns** | II | VIII | V |

| | |
|---|---|
| **Personality Characteristics** | Self-assertive, decisive, resourceful, active, action-oriented, enterprising, self-confident, talkative, energetic, forceful, ambitious, vigorous, adventurous, self-starting, moving, competitive, outspoken, initiating. **Energetic accomplisher—drives hard to achieve goals.** |
| **Relationship Behaviors** | Focus of attention on personal goals. Full dedication to winning. Never gives up. Expresses thoughts and feelings. Takes charge. Impatient to get into action. |
| **Vocational Talents** | Takes calculated risks. Gives leadership to practical projects. Starts new ventures. Tackles difficult challenges. Effective in personal sales. |
| **Wants Others To...** | Respond! "Don't just sit there – do something even if it's wrong." Say what you think – come on straight. Give loyalty and active support. "Lead, follow, or get out of the way." |

*Figure 5g*

# Pattern VIII

| Lead Strengths | Risking | Theoretical Thinking | Independent Risking |
|---|---|---|---|
| **Supporting Strengths** | Thinking | Practical Thinking | Dependent Risking |
| **Flex-patterns** | IV | VII | VI |
| **Personality Characteristics** | Dynamic, spirited, convincing, optimistic, dramatic, impulsive, imaginative, colorful, eloquent, innovative, versatile, exciting, charismatic, inspirational, enthusiastic, persuasive, impelling, exuberant. **Dynamic visionary—stimulates change.** | | |
| **Relationship Behaviors** | Focus of attention on own vision. Courage to risk all – "bet the farm." Wants to influence others. Seeks the spotlight. Enlivens relationships. Talks. | | |
| **Vocational Talents** | Gives dynamic leadership to a "cause." Sells a dream. Promotes an idea. Puts deals together. Public speaker. | | |
| **Wants Others To...** | Notice them and react. Show excitement and enthusiasm. Be influenced. Follow them. Be supportive. | | |

*Figure 5h*

# 3

# Innate Capacities

In the Power of Opposite Strengths, the second life force is identified as innate capacities. The purpose of this chapter is to define
the nature of this force and discuss its role in shaping human
personality.

Our innate capacities and our pattern of strengths are similar
in that both are genetically based. They are the two stable and enduring forces in our personality that determine our natural way
of being. These forces come into being at conception and maintain a constant shaping influence on our personalities throughout
our lifetimes.

These two stable forces also differ in a very significant way.
When we use our *Opposite Strength Inventories* to accurately
discover someone's pattern of strengths, we are attempting to
measure *how* the opposite strengths relate to one another in
forming a particular bundle of strengths in the personality core
within that individual. When psychologists or social scientists
measure innate capacities, on the other hand, they are concerned
with *how much* potential strength there is in the bundle as compared with other people. In other words, the pattern describes
the shape or configuration of the bundle itself, and innate capacities describe how much strength is within it when compared to
some external standard.

In general psychology, the force of innate capacities is dealt
with most fully in studies that deal with individual differences.
The principles and disciplines associated with tests and measurements are particularly important in this regard. Tests that

measure mental abilities, drive, or energy potential would all tend to measure what our Power of Opposite Strengths model refers to as innate capacities.

Throughout the development of the Power of Opposite Strengths, our focus has always been on the pattern of strengths—not on innate capacities. As a result, the Power of Opposite Strengths has much less to offer to a serious student who wants to learn about innate capacities and how to measure them. What the Power of Opposite Strengths *does* offer to such a student is a theory of personality that affirms the validity of individual differences in innate capacities and recognizes that these differences produce different personalities. Our other possible contribution is a better understanding of the basic nature of innate capacities—the understanding that these capacities do adhere to the Power of Opposite Strengths in their fundamental nature.

## Mental Abilities

Psychologists have been attempting to identify and measure the mental abilities of people for many years. Much progress has been made: Many different kinds of mental abilities have been identified, and many professionally validated tests have been designed to measure them.

Probably the best-known and most researched concept in the field of mental capacities is that of general intelligence. Alfred Benet did the pioneering work in 1905, and intelligence, as a specific capacity, has been studied extensively since that time.

One of the most vexing problems in trying to measure intelligence has been to devise a testing instrument that could measure the power of the brain itself as opposed to the quantity of knowledge it has absorbed. Many of the criticisms of so-called

"I.Q. tests" stem from the recognized difficulty of constructing a valid instrument that measures the innate capacity of the brain itself rather than the fruits of that capacity (knowledge).

The split-brain research of Nobel Prize-winner Roger Sperry and the related theories of the late Aleksandr Luria provide hope to those who are addressing the problems in measuring intelligence. Sperry's research has provided a radical new departure from the methodology that has dominated I.Q. testing since its beginning. The Kaufman Assessment Battery for Children (K-ABC) is a good example of a test using this new methodology.

Kaufman's three-part intelligence test is designed to measure how children process information, not what they already know. The focus is on the difference between sequential and simultaneous information processing. As Sperry confirmed in his prize-winning experiments, sequential processing tends to predominate in the brain's left hemisphere, and simultaneous processing tends to predominate in the right. In sequential processing, the brain solves a problem by dealing with information one bit at a time (similar to practical thinking in the Power of Opposite Strengths). Contrasted with this, simultaneous processing occurs when one integrates many stimuli at once (similar to theoretical thinking in the Power of Opposite Strengths). Sperry also assumes that while everyone uses both modes of thinking, one or the other—either sequential or simultaneous thinking—tends to be the dominant mode of thinking in some or most people.

The conclusions reached by Sperry in his split-brain research and the methodology used in such testing instruments as the K-ABC are very much in harmony with the Power of Opposite Strengths.

More recently, Dr. Howard Gardner has proffered a theory of multiple intelligences. Our understanding of this theory is that it is closely related to identifying the natural talents and aptitudes of

people with different natural patterns of strengths. More research
into this area is needed.

## Drive or Energy Potential

Far less work has been done in the area of scientifically measuring emotional drive. In recent years, considerable progress has
been made in measuring this important variable in our personalities. Further work needs to be done, however, before the nature
of drive is clearly understood and it can be most effectively mea-
sured in individuals.

In the Power of Opposite Strengths, we assume that the
amount of drive a person has is an innate capacity, along with
general intelligence. We also assume that the amount of drive
within individuals will be distributed along a normal probability
curve in much the same way as intelligence. Drive also seems to
have some relationship to the risking strength identified in the
Power of Opposite Strengths, but the nature of this relationship
is not yet clear. A great deal of work needs to be done before the
differences and similarities between these two constructs can be
clearly identified.

## Summary

In the last two chapters, the two stabilizing forces in our personality were discussed. They were identified as (1) our pattern of
strengths, and (2) our innate capacities. These two forces are
composed exclusively of strengths. They are inherently positive,
and there is nothing in their nature that can be regarded as negative or destructive to the creative process. Although we all pos-
sess the same strengths, we are different in that we have different
*patterns* of these strengths, and we also have different *amounts of*

these strengths. The Power of Opposite Strengths has no basis on which to evaluate these differences as either more or less desirable. Each of us has been given our own unique bundle of strengths. We need to feel good about our own bundle, whatever it maybe, and through its expression make our own unique contribution to the world.

In the next two chapters, the two dynamic forces that produce changes in our personalities will be discussed. They are (1) environment, and (2) personal choice. These two forces are *not* all positive. They can be expressed in constructive ways that release our creative potential, or they can be expressed in negative ways that interfere with and block out our natural creativeness. They are the two forces that determine how our pattern of strengths and innate capacities are expressed in the world. Through them, we enter the growth process that produces our personalities.

# 4

# Environment

This chapter deals with environmental influences, the third of the four forces that together produce the human personality. The environment has received much more attention from psychologists and social scientists than have the other three personality forces. It has been investigated more extensively, and much more is known about its specific effects on personality development. The best-known and most widely accepted psychological systems of our day tend to focus on the effects of the environment. Possibly *because* of the emphasis given to this force by professionals, the environment is commonly regarded as the dominant and most influential force that determines our personalities. This chapter presents a different view.

## Nature of the Environmental Force

Our environment is composed of external forces that are dynamic and in a constant state of flux. It is the only force shaping personality that is external to us. Our environment is created by outside sources. We ourselves are powerless to change it: All we can control is how we respond to it.

The environmental force is essentially an agent for change. If we are to continue our existence as individuals and as a species, we must adapt and adjust to the changing conditions in our environment. Our capacity to make flexible and adaptable responses to changing environmental conditions is what enables our survival.

Our changing environment demands that we exercise our adaptive capacities. In the process, we develop a creative human personality. It is important for our discussion here to note that being creative calls for a flexible, adaptive response to our environment, not a radical change in our basic make-up as individuals. To be more specific, responding creatively to our environment does not require a change in our structured pattern of strengths or a change in our innate capacities. It simply requires that we express our natural pattern of strengths and innate capacities in adaptive ways that fit the needs of a given situation.

Broadly speaking, the environmental forces that influence personality development can be classified into two main categories:

- natural forces

- forces that are set in motion by conscious human choices.

The natural forces in our environment are manifestations of the creative process at work in the universe. As such, they contribute in a positive way to the healthy development of each unique personality. Through the action of these natural forces, we are encouraged to fill our niche in the creative process and make our contribution to the whole. There is nothing negative or destructive about the natural forces in our environment.

In the Power of Opposite Strengths, a destructive force is defined as a force that is inhibitive to the creative process. It is a force that blocks or distorts the natural feeding process between our opposite strengths. This potential for turning a natural, positive force into a negative force is born with the advent of personal consciousness—the seat of our personal freedom to make conscious choices. People can make "good" conscious choices that contribute to the creative process, or they can make "bad" choices that are destructive to the process. These good and bad choices made by people create good and bad influences in our environment—influences that either contribute in a positive way to our personality development or are destructive to it.

The influence of particular personal choices can be passed on from generation to generation. This applies to both good choices and bad choices. There is a significant difference, however. Good choices maintain their influence because they are a living part of the creative process. Bad or destructive choices, on the other hand, may persist for a long time, but they will eventually die because they are not a contributing part of the creative process.

# How the Environmental Force Influences Personality Development

The environmental force begins its influence at the conception of an individual and is a continuing influence throughout the lifetime of that person. Although this influence varies at different times in a person's life, it is always there to some extent. We could not become individuals in the absence of an environment.

The natural environmental forces that affect us are wholly positive. They tend to guide us toward constructive expressions of our strengths within the creative process. The environment created by others, on the other hand, is a mixture of good and bad influences. Some environmental influences have a positive influence on our personality development, and sometimes they are inhibit or are destructive to our development.

The influences coming from others are especially potent in the development of our attitudes, value systems, and self-concepts. The extent to which we develop these characteristics in our early years is largely dependent upon how other people relate to us—especially those who are closest to us. Since we are all exposed to a mixture of good and bad influences coming from other people, these characteristics will always have some negative elements embedded within them. People who have a rich and nourishing environment with few negatives tend to develop attitudes that are more positive, sound value systems, and healthy self-concepts. Those who are exposed to an environment in which there are many negatives tend to develop attitudes that are more negative, inadequate value systems, and destructive self-concepts.

The attitudes, value systems, and self-concepts we develop in our formative years are not set for life, however. They can be changed by two of the life forces: a changing environment, and our personal choices. A new environment with more positive influences and good personal choices about how we think and behave tend to heal the wounds inflicted by earlier negative influences. Although the scars made by these early negatives will probably remain on our psyches, the wounds themselves can be healed with the help of a good environment and good personal choices.

Although all of us are affected to some extent by the environment that surrounds us, some seem to be affected more than others. Those who lean toward dependent risking in their natural pattern of strengths tend to be influenced more by environmental forces. Although they can and do exercise their power of personal choice, their environment tends to be the dominant influence in their personality development. For those who lean toward independent risking, the independent choices they make tend to be the dominant force in their personality development. They are still influenced by their environment, but their personal choices make a large difference in their development.

Not only does the influence of environment tend to vary with different individuals, but it also varies at different times with the same individual. At one time, the environment can be in the foreground and have the dominant influence on one's thinking and behavior. At other times, it may recede into the background and have the least effect. The environmental force is always there and having some effect, but the intensity of its influence is a dynamic variable, changing from moment to moment.

# Limitations of the Environmental Force

In the Power of Opposite Strengths, equal weight and potential influence is given to each of the four life forces. From a theoretical point of view, any of the four forces can have the dominant influence on a particular person. There is nothing within the forces themselves that would automatically or consistently make one more influential than another.

Since the actual influence of each of the forces varies with different individuals and at different times within the same individual, it is important for us to keep an open mind concerning the relative influence of these forces on a particular person. The Power of Opposite Strengths allows us to keep this open mind and helps us to resist the temptation to focus too sharply on only one or two of the forces while neglecting the others.

Although the effect of any one of the four life forces is necessarily moderated or limited by the other three forces, this section concentrates on exploring the limitations of the environmental force. We focus on the environment here because of the historical tendency to overemphasize its importance and consequently to de-emphasize the importance of the other three forces. Our intent is to challenge the practice of overemphasizing the influence of environmental factors in personality development and downplaying the influence of our pattern of strengths, innate capacities, and personal choices. The intent is not to depreciate the influence of environment, but rather to place it on an equal par with the others and give all four equal statuses.

The influence of our environment is limited by the stable structure inherent in our pattern of strengths. The stabilizing forces that are a part of the creative process produce a stable bundle of strengths at the core of every personality. This stabilizing force tends to keep the structure of the natural pattern intact, regardless of changes in the outside environment. With continued advances in genetic engineering, more skill will likely be developed in altering genetic material. It is conceivable that, in the future, it may become possible to change the genetic structures that produce a particular pattern of strengths. Even if this is done, however, it will not lessen the stabilizing power of the new genetic structure on personality. The force will simply be expressed through a new, stable, and structured form. We may alter the forms through which the stabilizing forces are expressed, but the forces themselves remain untouched.

The influence of our environment is also limited by the stabilizing forces in nature that create the genetic structures which give uniqueness to our innate capacities. Again, genetic engineering may find effective ways to alter the genetic materials associated with innate capacities. Even if this happens, however, the stabilizing force of genetic structure will remain. It may manifest itself through changed genetic structures, but it will still bring stability and constancy to our personalities. The important point to remember is that stability and structure are just as much parts of our personalities as are dynamism and change.

Our freedom to make personal choices serves as a third distinct limitation to the influence of environmental forces. To put it quite simply, we have the power to choose how we allow a particular environment to influence us. An example that illustrates this power readily comes to mind.

In his work as a coaching psychologist to management, Jay Thomas frequently interviews managers in an effort to understand them as individuals. During these interviews, he routinely asks them to tell him about the people who have had the greatest influence in their lives. Usually they talk about people who were good models for them, or about people who encouraged them in some way. In some instances, however, a very different thing happens, and the manager talks about a father or mother who set a bad example. Frequently it is a father who was an alcoholic and turned out to be a dismal failure, both as a husband and as a father. The surprising thing is that the manager has usually learned from the bad example set by his or her father and turned a very negative environment into a positive learning experience. Sometimes the interviewee actually expresses gratitude to the father for showing what *not* to do in life.

A negative environment does not automatically have a negative influence. Some people, through personal choice, make lemonade out of a lemon.

All psychological systems tend to focus on one or two of the four life forces. Although the Power of Opposite Strengths recognizes and places an equal value on each of the four forces, our application of the Power of Opposite Strengths tends to focus on two of the forces: our pattern of strengths, and our freedom to make personal choices.

Most of the best-known systems of our day focus on the two dynamic forces: the environmental force, and our freedom to make personal choices. One of the most popular—behaviorism—focuses exclusively on the effects of the environment. The danger inherent in focusing on one or two of the forces is that this can be interpreted to mean these one or two forces are consistently more important and influential in forming the personality. This tends to create a value system in which one or two of the forces are valued above the others.

This philosophical position is at odds with the Power of Opposite Strengths. When any of the four forces are depreciated or disregarded, the result is a view that is destructive to normal and healthy personality development. As an example, when the influence of environment is depreciated, it lessens our awareness of the important influence we can have on each other through social interaction.

The destructive effects of overemphasizing the environmental force come from the de-emphasis and neglect of the influences that come from the other three forces. When our natural pattern of strengths is disregarded, everyone looks the same. Locke, an English philosopher, expressed this view many years ago in the statement, "At birth a person is a *tabula rasa* and through experience becomes whatever is writ on this blank sheet." In other words, Locke posited that the environment is the sole determinant of our individuality. It is hard to imagine how much destructiveness has resulted from such a statement.

When we disregard our unique bundles of opposite strengths, we lose our stamps of self-identify as people. We become copies of each other rather than our original and unique selves. We become pieces of putty to be molded into shapes that fit someone else's idea of what we should be, rather than unique people with destinies and particular vocations to fulfill. We lose our individuality and our dignity as significant human beings.

## Summary

This chapter has presented a discussion of the environmental force—one of the four forces that produce a healthy personality. Environment was defined as an external force that either contributes to healthy personality development or is destructive to it. Whatever destructive elements may be in the environment were seen as coming from the bad personal choices made by people. Environmental influences were seen as having a major effect on the formation of our attitudes, value systems, and self-concepts.

This chapter also discussed the limitations of the environmental force, primarily to counteract the overemphasis placed on the environmental force by the most influential psychological systems of our day. The intent was not to depreciate the important place of the environment in personality development, but to place it on an equal par with the other three forces.

# 5

# Personal Choice

This chapter describes the fourth and last life force that determines the human personality: our power to make personal choices. It has a special relationship to the other three personality forces in that it is produced by the other three. Our power to make personal choices results from the creative interaction of our opposite strengths, our innate capacities, and a nourishing environment.

The force of personal choice is similar to the environmental force in that it produces changes—especially in the direction of people's thinking and behavior. It is different from the environmental force in that personal choice is internal and is controlled by the individual, whereas the environment is external and is controlled by outside sources.

## Nature of Personal Choice

As our opposite strengths feed each other, they produce an increasing degree of personal awareness. When this awareness reaches a particular level, we experience personal consciousness, and this consciousness is what creates our freedom to make personal choices. We do not choose this freedom. It is thrust on us by the creative interaction of the strengths within us. Although we are not responsible for the creation of our freedom to choose, we *are* accountable for the personal choices we make after we receive the power to choose.

When we develop consciousness and gain the power to make personal choices, we become conscious participants in the process of creation. This is both an opportunity and a responsibility. Either the personal choices that we make contribute to the creative process at work in the world, or they work against it. This is what defines good and bad personal choices. Good choices feed and enhance the creative process, and bad choices distort and restrict the process.

Our power of personal choice gives us the ability to choose our focus of attention and to control our behavior. Although the other three life forces limit this ability, it is still a very real power in our lives and in our development. In many ways, this power to make conscious choices appears to be an evolutionary development that enables us to respond in more flexible and adaptive ways to our environment. For example, if we focus our attention on the creative process, we can better understand how it works, and, by directing our behavior in line with its demands, we can participate in it more fully.

# How Personal Choices Influence Personality Development

Our personal choices make a difference in who we become. If we make good choices that are in harmony with the creative process, we tend to mature and develop a healthy personality. If we make bad choices that go against the process, our personality tends to deteriorate and become a destructive force.

Our personal choices also make a difference in how we affect the people around us. If we make good choices, we tend to encourage others to develop into healthy personalities. If we make bad choices, we tend to become a negative and destructive influence on others.

Much of what the Power of Opposite Strengths has to offer comes from its concepts regarding how the creative process works and the specific choices we must make to participate more fully within it. The nature of those specific choices and what we must do to make them is the primary subject matter in Part II (Being Flexible) and Part III (Sustained Success in Relationships) of the Opposite Strengths Seminar.

# Limitations of the Power of Personal Choice

As with all of the life forces, the power of personal choice is limited by the power of the other three forces. The influence of our personal choices may be great, or it may be small—it depends on the person and the situation. No matter how powerful the influence of our personal choices may become, however, it will never become strong enough to totally overcome or do away with the power of the other three life forces.

Our power to change through personal choice is limited by the stabilizing power of the genetic structures that give form and intensity to our natural pattern of strengths. We cannot become anything we want to become simply by thinking and changing our behavior. We can modify the ways in which our pattern is expressed in the world, but we cannot, through the power of personal choice, do away with the stabilizing power of our pattern of strengths.

Our power to make personal choices is also limited by the forces that create our environment. Within limits, we can modify the form and structure of our environment, we can remove ourselves from one environment and place ourselves in another, and we can choose how we will respond to a particular environment. However, the forces that actually create our environment are largely beyond our control. Most of our ability to affect our environment comes through the exercise of our personal choice.

# Applying Opposite Strengths in Your Life

By receiving Opposite Strengths Executive Coaching or attending an Opposite Strengths Seminar, you are receiving the best guidance available in learning how to apply Opposite Strengths to your personal and professional lives. I have personally trained each Opposite Strengths Certified Executive Coach and Certified Facilitator.

It is now time for you to put down this book and go to our Web site, *www.oppositestrengths.com*. There, through the online *Guide to Being Yourself* report (which is based on the *Opposite Strengths Inventories* completed on you), you can now add to your understanding of the experience of the executive coaching you are receiving or your experience of Part I of the Opposite Strengths Seminar–Being Yourself. You already completed some Opposite Strengths Inventories–most likely one Self-report and around five Other-reports. You should have completed one Self-report *Inventory* and at least five Other-report *Inventories*. But if you haven't, don't worry. You can complete as many Opposite Strengths Inventories as you wish at any time you want. At any time you can ask your Opposite Strengths Certified Executive Coach or Opposite Strengths Certified Facilitator to show you how.

You have already joined our online community by taking Opposite Strengths Executive Coaching or being enrolled in an Opposite Strengths Seminar and completing the Opposite Strengths Inventories. You can log on to your Member Home Page on our Web site using your Member ID and Member

Password, which were given to you previously (your Opposite Strengths Certified Executive Coach or Facilitator can give you that information if you don't have it).

Why are Other-report *Inventories* important? There are two reasons:  1) it's helpful and interesting to you to see how others perceive you, and 2) Other-report *Inventories* increase the accuracy in identifying your natural pattern of strengths. So I encourage you to complete as many Other-report *Inventories* as you wish.

Who should complete the Other-report *Inventories* on you? Those people generally fall in one of three categories: 1) people you work with, 2) your friends and social acquaintances, and 3) family including spouse. Here's a bit of help for you.

- Think of people you would like to have complete Other-report *Inventories* on you and jot down their name and e-mail addresses here:

Name                                    E-mail address

1. _____

2. _____

3. _____

4. _____

5. _____

6. _____

7. _____

8. _____

9. _____

10. _____

- Go to our Web site, *www.oppositestrengths.com*, and log on by entering your Member ID and Member Password.

  My Member ID:

  My Member Password:

- After you log on, you will be taken to your personal Member Home Page. To have additional Other-report *Inventories* completed on you, look under the heading "Opposite Strengths Inventories," and click on the link "Ask someone to complete an Inventory on me." Then follow the instructions to request more Other-report *Inventories*.

- Now go to the upper left corner of your Member Home Page. You will see a heading entitled "Opposite Strengths Guides." Click on *"Guide to Being Yourself."* Your custom *Guide to Being Yourself* will pop up in a separate window. There is both a Preview (short version) and Full Report (long version).

At the end of Part II of this book, I'll introduce you to the next online Guide available to you – the *Guide to Being Flexible*. But don't read that now. First use your Opposite Strengths Executive Coaching or Opposite Strengths Seminar experience to get a clear understanding of your lead and supporting strengths – your natural pattern of strengths – through the Analysis of Strengths you've already received and the online *Guide to Being Yourself* you just generated from our Web site. Then you'll be ready to learn about flexibility. Now, please read on!

—Dr. Tommy Thomas

# Transition

Up to this point, we have been focusing on the fundamentals of the Power of Opposite Strengths. In the Introduction, we discussed principles of the Power of Opposite Strengths. In Part I, the first chapter presented the Power of Opposite Strengths, and the next four chapters discussed each of the four forces that shape our lives. For the most part, the basic concepts of the Power of Opposite Strengths have been presented. In Parts II and III, we will turn our attention to how these concepts may be put to practical use.

Part II deals with how we grow and mature as individuals by being flexible in the use of our strengths. It describes the growth process, discusses our tendencies and temptations, shows how we can become polarized, and identifies the growth choices we can make to take us toward personal maturity.

Part III is about understanding other people and the relationship dynamics between people. It describes what is going on in a creative relationship between two people, discusses four distinct relationship tendencies that human beings experience, identifies the relationship characteristics each pattern tends to produce, and gives general guidance on strengthening relationships with others.

# PART II
## Being Flexible

# 6

# The Growth Process

The original impetus for the development of the Power of Opposite Strengths came from Jay Thomas's efforts to understand the process of growth (see the Introduction). His desire to understand this process has remained the central driving force behind the development of the Power of Opposite Strengths. The breakthrough concept of opposite strengths was the first fruit of his efforts, and it continues to be the cornerstone of our view of the growth process. The model of growth presented here is grounded in the principles presented in the earlier discussion on the Power of Opposite Strengths. The intent in this chapter is to build on the Power of Opposite Strengths and show how the growth process works in personality development. The growth process and the creative process are interchangeable terms in the Power of Opposite Strengths—they point toward the same process. Although we have chosen to use the term "growth process" in this presentation, "creative process" or "success process" could be used just as well.

## Fundamental Forces in the Growth Process

Understanding the concepts of growth and flexibility in the Power of Opposite Strengths requires us to distinguish between the activity of the strength itself and the product of that activity. In the basic pair of opposite strengths, our thinking activities produce mental perceptions, and our risking activities produce feelings. In the thinking pair, practical thinking activity results in perceptions of reality. We see the facts, how things really are. On the other hand, theoretical thinking activity yields perceptions of possibilities and allows us to understand ideas and have a vision of how things could be.

In the risking pair of strengths, risking dependence allows us to experience the support and approval of others and build warm relationships. When we risk independence, we experience personal freedom and power and develop self-confidence. The six opposite strengths and the particular product each strength produces are summarized in Figure 6.

The six opposite strengths and their products are the fundamental forces that power the growth process. The opposite strengths themselves are continuously active and, for the most part, unconscious. The activity of these opposite strengths produces our conscious awareness. We are conscious of our mental perceptions and our feelings, but we are largely unaware of the activity that produces these perceptions and feelings.

The fundamental forces in the growth process are wholly positive. There are no negative forces within the process itself. A person may relate to these fundamental forces in a negative way, but the forces themselves are inherently positive. Each force makes its own positive contribution to the process.

# How the Growth Process Results in Personal Growth

The growth process works within us through the creative interaction between the two opposite strengths in each pair. The activity of the opposite strengths is natural and automatic. Each strength produces its own natural fruit, and it feeds on the fruit produced by its opposite. This symbiotic or synergistic

# The Success Process

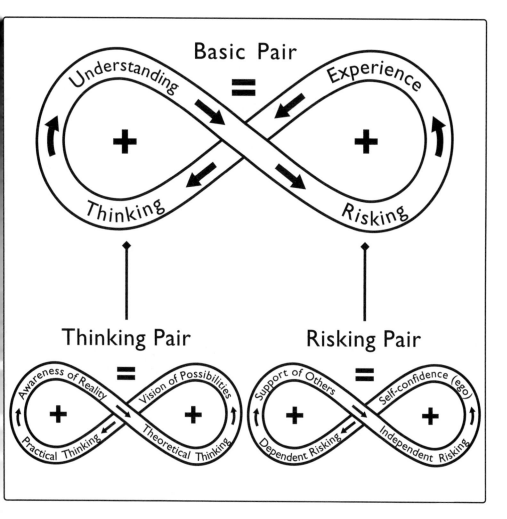

*Figure 6*

interaction is what permits the increase we experience in growth. As a strength produces more fruit, more raw materials are available for its opposite strength to use in producing even more of its own fruit. Note that what increases during growth is the product or fruit of the strength, not the strength itself. This is in harmony with our original assumption that our pattern of strengths and our innate capacities are constants in our lives.

In the growth process, both opposite strengths in a pair remain active and become more productive through their inter-dependent, feeding relationship. In other words, when we grow, we garner additional strength on *both* sides of a pair of opposite strengths. We have clearer perceptions and experience more courage to risk. We perceive reality more clearly and are more aware of alternatives. We experience stronger relationships with others and feel more self-confidence. This approach to growth affirms the idea that the two opposite strengths operate to-gether, each one fueling the other. If the activity of either one is blocked, it reduces the fruit that both can produce. The two strengths either grow together or decay together. Neither one can operate by itself.

This view of growth is contrary to the way most of us tend to think about how we can become stronger on one side of a pair of opposite strengths. For example, most people would accept the following statement as true: "One becomes more independent by being less dependent; one becomes more practical by being less theoretical; one becomes more of a risker by being less of a thinker." Sometimes this negative approach is expressed in personal evaluations such as, "You are too dependent," or "You are too theoretical."

There are at least two things wrong with statements such as these. First, they imply that a good strength is really a weakness.

Second, they suggest that people grow by blocking and fighting against a positive strength.

In contrast with the negative approach described above, the Power of Opposite Strengths affirms the positive value of every one of our strengths. It also encourages the natural expression of all our strengths as an essential requirement for personal growth. What allows us to take this positive approach is the concept that distinguishes the activity of a strength from the product this activity produces. Growth does require that we give up something and make sacrifices, however. Healthy, growing people learn that we must pay the price: There are no free lunches.

Conventional wisdom recognizes that we must give up something in growth. That is what is behind the idea that we grow by blocking a strength. The mistake is in the belief that when we grow, we give up the activity of a strength. The truth is that what we actually give up in growth is the *fruit* of the strength—not the natural activity of the strength itself.

Here is an illustration of how we grow by sacrificing the fruit of a strength rather than consciously blocking the activity of a strength. Consider people who have a natural lead strength in dependence. Out of being themselves, they naturally develop support and approval from others. This support and approval is a valued fruit of dependent risking, and it usually means a good deal to these people, who naturally tend to favor dependent risking over independent risking.

It is also natural for people who have dependence as a lead strength to develop a perceived need for more self-confidence—which of course is the fruit of *independent* risking. In using the Power of Opposite Strengths, we encourage those people to affirm their dependent strength as a good strength that produces valuable results, and not to consciously fight against or block out their natural inclination to be dependent. We avoid saying, "You are too dependent," or "You have to stop being so dependent on other people." Rather, we take a positive approach and suggest that they consciously shift emphasis to a more active expression of their independent strength.

We also try to help people who have dependence as a lead strength understand that becoming more active in expressing independence may require them to give up some of the support and approval they are now receiving from others. Nevertheless, they must stand ready to make this sacrifice. We give this advice with the conviction that standing ready to sacrifice the support and approval of others can free up a stronger expression of independence and result in an experience of personal growth. Their growth manifests itself in their behavior as a stronger expression of *both* dependence and independence. They also experience more self-confidence and more support and approval from others—the fruits of *both* independence and dependence. By sacrificing the support and approval of others to the process, they actually receive more support and approval in the future. To stay in the process, they must also sacrifice the additional support and approval that they will receive in the future.

The goal is to live in the process, not to indulge ourselves in our fruits. This requires a continuing sacrifice of the fruits that we produce.

## Participation in the Growth Process

The primordial force that creates all existence expresses itself in the growth process described in the preceding section. This force creates us—we are natural participants in the process. We are not the process ourselves, nor do we create on our own apart from the process. The process was here before we came into being as individuals and will continue to exist after we die. We were created to give all we have to the process.

Although we are natural participants in the growth process, with the advent of human consciousness our participation took on a new dimension. Now it becomes a matter of human choice—both our own personal choice and the choices made by other people. With the emergence of our own personal consciousness, we must *choose* to participate in the growth process. No longer is it simply natural and automatic. Now we must make some hard choices and be willing to pay the price. Once this power to choose is thrust upon us, there is no turning back. We cannot choose not to choose. Any effort to get rid of consciousness is still a personal choice that affects our participation in the process.

The conscious choices we make are either good or bad. They are good choices when they contribute to the growth process, and they are bad choices when they fight against or block the process. The better we understand the process and our role in it, the better equipped we can be to make good choices. The remainder of this section is devoted to a discussion of three basic choices that determine the extent of our participation in the growth process and the development of our individual potential.

Our first choice is between being ourselves and trying to be something we aren't. The choice to be true to our natural way of being makes us participants in the growth process. The choice to reject our natural way and try to be something different makes us phony and takes us out of the process.

All of us have our own unique bundle of strengths at the core, and this bundle of opposite strengths gives us a niche to fill in the creative process. The constant demand of the growth process is for us to fill our niche by contributing in ways that fit our natural strengths.

In the Power of Opposite Strengths, the eight patterns of strengths are used as conceptual tools to help people identify their natural ways of being. What makes us participants in the growth process is the choice to express our pattern, whatever it may be. Although the Power of Opposite Strengths holds that the eight patterns have equal value and that all are required by the creative process, this is not necessarily the value system held by the society in which we live. In most societies, some patterns are valued more highly than others are, and the favored pattern can vary from one society to another. If our own natural pattern happens to be in disfavor in our own society, we are under a good deal of pressure to show a different pattern and hide our real selves. This is a hard choice. To be accepted by others, we must be something other than what we really are, but to be participants in the growth process, we must be ourselves and risk the rejection of others.

The same problem also crops up in sexual stereotypes. Men are expected to show certain patterns of strengths, and women are expected to show other patterns. When people discover that their natural patterns do not fit the stereotype held by their culture, they have to make a painful choice about their behavior. On the one hand, they are rejected if they don't fit the mold, and on the other hand, they lose themselves if they try to be something they aren't.

How does a person solve this dilemma in a creative way? We will give a short answer here and reserve a more complete answer for the discussion in Chapter 9 entitled *Personal Growth*. The short answer is that people having this problem need to go ahead and be themselves and risk the rejection that is likely to come. At the same time, they need to be flexible enough to use their supporting strengths to deal with the problems caused by being themselves.

Our second choice has to do with being flexible and deliberately emphasizing the strengths required by differing situations. In a sense, it is the polar opposite of being true to ourselves. Here we must consciously choose to be true to a situation and express the strength that will further the growth process in that particular situation. This adaptation is a creative response to our environment.

A personal example from Jay Thomas's life illustrates the nature of this choice. His natural way of being is to lead with theoretical thinking and emphasize theory rather than the practical application of the theory. When he started giving seminars on the Power of Opposite Strengths in 1966, he gave presentations in the way that was natural for him: they were highly theoretical and conceptual. During these early years, after he had presented a seminar to a group of bank executives, the bank president gently chided him, saying, "Jay, I really think you have some good ideas, but it seems to me that you overkill them."

The comment got Jay's attention, and he began to reflect on his presentation style. It became painfully obvious to him that his lectures were highly theoretical and very abstract. To practical managers, they were undoubtedly dull and boring. The bank president had indicated that Jay needed to be more practical and talk about how his ideas could be put to practical use in solving some of their management problems. Jay then had a choice to make. He could continue to emphasize theory out of his natural leanings, or he could adapt to the needs of his audiences and bring more practicality to his presentations. Since his livelihood was dependent upon having successful seminars, he decided to change his lectures by giving additional practical examples and talking about ways to put his concepts to practical use in solving personnel and customer relations problems.

Immediately, Jay found that his seminars became more lively, effective, and useful. In addition, shifting emphasis to his practical thinking strength had the effect of giving him a better grasp on reality. In turn, this concentration on factual data gave him more raw materials to use in developing an even better theory. His adaptive response had put him in the growth process. As Jay notes, "I could have chosen to blame my audiences for not having enough interest in theory and continued to overkill my ideas, but I suspect that eventually would have led to my giving lectures to empty rooms."

At first blush, it may appear that the choice to be one's natural self and to emphasize one's supporting strengths is in conflict—that you can't do both. However, in the Power of Opposite Strengths, this is precisely what mature people do well. The flavor of their natural way is unmistakable and is always there, but at the same time, they show flexibility in expressing the strength required by the situation, even if it happens to be one of their supporting strengths.

Our third choice has to do with the sacrifice we must make when we choose to be ourselves, and when we choose to be flexible and adapt to the situation. In both instances, we must give up something that has great personal value to us. The growth process requires that we give up the fruits of our strengths and let them be used up in the creative process. Our choice is either to give them up to the process or to hang on to them for our personal use. If we choose to give up these valued fruits and invest them in the creative process, we become participants in the process. If we choose to indulge ourselves in these fruits and refuse to let them go, we take ourselves out of the process.

This choice to sacrifice our fruits is painful because it involves giving up those things that have the most value to us. Jay Thomas offers himself as an example. His best products are his ideas (which come from his natural lead strength—theoretical thinking) and his self-confidence or ego (which comes from his lead strength in independent risking). His ideas are very dear to him, and he has a tremendous ego investment in them. The hard choice he must make if he is to be involved in the creative process is to put the ideas out into the world and let them be tested by reality.

The threat he feels is that his ideas might be wrong and be found wanting. If so, he stands to lose something that has great value to him, and his ego will be bruised.

The growth process, however, demands that he make the sacrifice. If he indulges himself in his ideas and refuses to let them be used up in the creative process, he will become polarized on his own ideas and take himself out of the growth process. Not only would that take him out of the process, but he would also become involved in a process that is the opposite of growth—a process of psychological decay. On the other hand, if he chooses to make the sacrifice, he puts himself in the growth process and positions himself to have greater practical effectiveness and to have new and even better ideas in the future.

# 7

# Personal Tendencies

A personal tendency is an inclination to favor a particular strength in a pair of opposite strengths. We all have tendencies. They are a natural part of being human. They need to be understood, affirmed, and expressed. They also need to be dealt with when they get us into trouble and cause us pain. In the Power of Opposite Strengths, we do not seek to get rid of our personal tendencies. If we did, we would get rid of our selves and our distinctiveness as individual persons. We should seek only to become aware of our tendencies and gain skill in dealing with the problems they bring about.

We have two kinds of tendencies:

- natural tendencies
- learned tendencies.

Our natural tendencies come from our natural pattern of strengths. We naturally favor our lead strengths, and this bias will express itself naturally in our personal tendencies. Many of our tendencies come from our natural way of being—how we are put together within us.

Our learned tendencies come from our interactions with our environment, particularly those with other people. Although our parents and the society that nurtured us have taught us many valuable and good things, much of what we have learned has been imperfect, incomplete, and one-sided. Other people have given us many of our prejudices, a good deal of inaccurate information, and a number of wrong ideas. We all experience many distortions in our personal value system because of what we have been taught by others. Many of our tendencies to regard one strength as more valuable than its opposite have come from a poorly conceived value system that we have picked up from other people.

Sometimes a learned tendency can be in opposition to a natural tendency. Here is an example that illustrates this fact. A professor at a Southwestern university used the Power of Opposite Strengths to discover he had the Pattern III combination of natural lead strengths. He naturally favored theoretical thinking, but he felt that he actually favored practical thinking. In reflecting upon his earlier years, it became apparent that he had a natural tendency to favor theoretical thinking, but the West Texas culture in which he grew up so depreciated theory and put so much emphasis on practicality that he had developed a learned tendency to favor practicality.

Developing this learned tendency to favor practicality did not change the professor's basic nature, but it did rob him of some of his sense of self-worth. As he became acquainted with the Power of Opposite Strengths and developed a greater appreciation for his natural bent toward theoretical thinking, his sense of self-worth increased, and he became more productive by feeling freer to express his theoretical thinking. The learned tendency to depreciate his theoretical thinking is still with him, but its negative effect has been lessened.

The most mature and effective people are aware of their tendencies and usually develop a sense of humor regarding them. Jay Thomas first became aware of this through his interviews with business managers. During those interviews, he would usually ask the executives to tell him the most important lesson they had learned during their lives. He discovered that those who were the most mature would rather quickly tell him about what they had learned. Often, they would say it with a distinctive smile, acknowledging that they had both realized and accepted something about themselves.

Often, the lesson mentioned was learning the importance of listening to other people. Usually the executives wanted to talk about how they had learned the lesson, and in doing so, they would talk about their natural tendency to talk when they should be listening. To Jay's surprise, many of them went on to offer good-natured remarks such as, "Actually, I'm not sure how well I really learned that lesson. I *still* talk too much and don't listen enough."

Having this kind of experience over and over again with psychologically healthy people brought Jay to his first realization that mature, growing people do have natural tendencies they really never get rid of. What they learn to do is to accept these tendencies as a natural part of who they are and develop skill in dealing with them when they cause problems. This seems to involve a relaxed acceptance of their tendencies and an ability to laugh at themselves.

Figure 6 presents a list of common tendencies that normal, healthy people experience. As you read these tendencies, you probably will find that you experience a number of them. During our seminars on the Power of Opposite Strengths, we ask the participants to read this list of tendencies and circle those they feel fit them. Most people circle from five to fifteen tendencies.

We enter the creative process by being ourselves—by being who we were created to be as unique, imperfect, out-of-balance persons. In this way, we find our place and make our own unique contribution to the whole.

In the terminology of the Power of Opposite Strengths, we are being ourselves when we express our natural tendencies, and the first step in entering the growth process is to follow our natural tendencies. Mature people go ahead and show who they are by following their natural tendencies, in spite of the realization

# Common Tendencies

## Tendency to...

1. ... talk when it's time to listen.
2. ... avoid confrontation and conflict when it's time to express real thoughts and feelings.
3. ... say "yes" when it's time to say "no."
4. ... withdraw into own self-sufficiency when it's time to draw on the strengths of others.
5. ... imagine the possibilities when it's time to get the facts.
6. ... wait for the other person to make the first move when it's time to take the initiative.
7. ... compete with others when it's time to be cooperative.
8. ... hold on to established ways when it's time to change and try new things.
9. ... stay emotionally involved when it's time to back off and be more objective.
10. ... go along with others when it's time to go your own way.
11. ... think about problems when it's time to look for solutions.
12. ... make the decision when it's time to think more before deciding.
13. ... hold feelings inside when it's time to express them more openly.
14. ... drive hard to accomplish own goals when it's time to find out what others are thinking and feeling.
15. ... think about theory when it's time to be practical.
16. ... depend on others when it's time to depend on yourself.
17. ... do things personally when it's time to trust others to do them.
18. ... be sympathetic and supportive when it's time to require others to be more responsible.
19. ... change things when it's time to hold steady and keep things as they are.
20. ... emphasize the realities when it's time to emphasize the possibilities.
21. ... be impatient with others when it's time to be more understanding of others.
22. ... do things that please others when it's time to pay more attention to own needs and desires.
23. ... be quiet and listen when it's time to speak out.
24. ... take risks when it's time to take fewer chances.
25. ... speculate about future possibilities when it's time to look at present realities.
26. ... think own thoughts when it's time to listen to what others are saying.
27. ... analyze the problem when it's time to take action.
28. ... assertively express thoughts and feelings when it's time to be more reserved and quiet.
29. ... be tolerant of others when it's time to be more firm with others.
30. ... be practical and realistic when it's time to be more imaginative.

*Figure 7*

that at some point they will develop a problem with the outside world. In other words, healthy, growing people go through life "at a tilt," and this is what keeps them vital and effective.

The second step in living creatively is to deal effectively with the pains and problems that naturally come to us as a result of following our natural tendencies. Our awareness of the problems our tendencies can cause and our skill in dealing creatively with these problems is just as much a part of our maturity as is being true to ourselves.

We can polarize on either of these two steps and take ourselves out of the creative process. We can become so intent on being ourselves that we fail to develop skill in being flexible and adapting to our environment. On the other hand, we can become so flexible and adaptable that we lose ourselves. When we continue to do one without the other, we enter a process of psychological decay. This process tends to feed on itself and become increasingly destructive and painful until we make the painful choices required to break polarization.

Chapter 8 describes this process of polarization and how we experience its destructive effects.

# 8

# Polarization

Although the Power of Opposite Strengths is a positive psychology that views strengths as the fundamental building blocks of the personality, it does affirm the reality of negative and destructive forces in human life. We believe that these negative forces come into existence with the advent of human consciousness— the source of our power to make conscious choices about how we think and behave. The nature of these negative and destructive forces is understood through the concept of polarization, which is the subject of this chapter.

While we will be dealing with the topic of negative and destructive forces in this chapter, we do not want to give the impression that proven therapeutic techniques have been developed for using the Power of Opposite Strengths with people who are severely disabled, either mentally or emotionally. The concept of polarization presented here has gradually emerged out of our experiences working with psychologically healthy people. We were not trained as nor have we practiced as clinical psychologists or psychiatrists. On those occasions when we find ourselves in professional relationships with people who appear to be in need of therapy, it is our practice to refer them to other professionals who are competent to deal with illness. We are hopeful, however, that the basic concepts of the Power of Opposite Strengths, including those regarding polarization, can make a contribution to a better understanding of what may be going on within a person who is severely disturbed psychologically. We enthusiastically encourage others to carry out research and develop techniques for using the Power of Opposite Strengths to combat mental and emotional illness.

# The Creative Process Within

Our opposite strengths naturally interact and feed each other creatively in an orderly process. This creative interaction between our opposite strengths goes on all the time, as long as we are alive. Let's look at this process as it occurs naturally within us.

Although we could start with any of our strengths, for the sake of illustration, let's start with practical thinking. As our practical thinking strength is active, we become aware of a problem in reality. This automatically stimulates an emphasis on our theoretical thinking to look for a possible solution. These two kinds of thinking, working creatively together, produce a clear perception of the problem and a concept of what we need to do to solve it. The creative perception gives us confidence, and this confidence gives us courage to move into action.

Let's speculate about how the process may work on the risking side. We may start with an expression of independence. In expressing independence, we separate from others and experience a sense of personal freedom and self-worth. Before long, however, we experience this separation as painful and feel a need to relate to other human beings. Out of this need, we seek to be with other people. In these relationships, our dependent risking strength becomes more active, and its expression results in an experience of support and approval from others. Out of the creative interaction of independence and dependence, we experience both more self-worth and stronger supporting relationships from others. This gives us greater basic confidence. In turn, that confidence allows us to face the reality of problems more directly and also to dream bigger dreams.

This is admittedly a somewhat simplistic description of a very complex process. The goal it to communicate two key points:

- the creative process goes on naturally within each of us
- all we need to do is make the conscious choices that keep our strengths naturally interacting and contributing to this creative process.

Every human being is creative within. The positive strengths in the personality core naturally feed each other in a continuous process of creation. How do negatives enter into this process? They enter when one of the strengths in a pair of opposite strengths is blocked. This blockage sets up a process of psychological decay within the individual that becomes increasingly painful with the passage of time. This process is referred to as "polarization." We get stuck on one side and continue to emphasize one strength while, at the same time, we block the expression of strength in its polar opposite.

There are two forces that take us toward polarization. One force comes from the negative influences in our environment. The other comes from the innate, out-of-balance nature that all human beings share.

One of the most common negative environmental influences is being taught a value system in which one of our strengths is depreciated or perhaps even regarded as a negative. A learned negative view of one of our positive strengths tends to cause us to block its expression. Doing so takes us out of the creative process and moves us toward polarization. Just how far it moves us depends on how severely we block the expression of the positive strength.

The negative influences in our environment that tend to take us toward polarization are very important, and becoming aware of them can be helpful in our efforts to deal with them creatively.

In spite of the importance of becoming aware of these negative environmental influences, the focus in the Power of Opposite Strengths is on the personal choices we can make *after* we become aware of the influence our environment is having on us.

Our own out-of-balance makeup is manifested most basically in our pattern of strengths. It is natural for us to favor our lead strengths and express these strengths more strongly than we do our supporting strengths. This being the case, we tend to be more aware of the good fruits coming from our lead strengths, and, out of this awareness, we tend to polarize more frequently on the fruits of our lead strengths.

For example, a person who has independent risking as one of his or her natural lead strengths likely has a tendency to experience and enjoy the values of being alone. Because of this, there is a strong temptation to withdraw from other people. To say it in another way, the person enjoys the values of being alone so much that he or she is tempted to disregard or depreciate the values of being involved with other people. On the other hand, people who have a natural lead strength in dependent risking may have an opposite tendency and temptation. They may enjoy the values of being with people so much that they are tempted to avoid being alone.

We do not want to give the impression that we tend to polarize only on the fruits of our lead strengths. In reality, we can polarize on any of our strengths—even if they are our supporting strengths. Our environmental situation may place such a demand on the expression of our supporting strengths that we become more aware of their good fruits and, as a result, we have a tendency to polarize on our supporting strengths.

We can also polarize on one strength and then later make a switch and become polarized on the opposite strength. We can shift back and forth, alternately polarizing on one then the other, never really blending the strengths in creative interaction. When this happens, the two strengths become disassociated and function separately, rather than as a creative whole. This alternating shift from one strength to its opposite without the integrity of blending may be one explanation of what is going on in some types of personality disorders (particularly in the manic-depressive disorder that has come to be known as bipolar disorder).

# The Results of Polarization

Our negative feelings and distorted perceptions come out of the polarization process. Since we live in an environment that has some negative influences, and we all have natural tendencies that take us into the early stages of polarization, it is normal to experience some negative feelings and distorted perceptions. This is human nature.

It is the *extent* of polarization that determines our maturity and quality of life. The more polarized we become, the more we experience such negative feelings as depression, fear, guilt, anxiety, resentment, hostility, jealousy, inferiority, and despair. Not only do our negative feelings become more intense as polarization deepens, but our perceptions become even more distorted. As our negative feelings and distorted perceptions intensify, we experience a corresponding increase in the pain associated with them. In turn, the increasing pain of polarization becomes a motivating force that tends to turn us back to creativity and psychological health.

Although the increasing problems and pain associated with the polarization process create a motivating force tending to turn us toward growth, they are never enough to do the job alone. We must sacrifice the fruits on which we are polarized and change our thinking and behavior through a conscious personal choice before we can break polarization. This sacrifice and change of thinking and behavior is what relieves our pain and puts us back in the creative process.

# Becoming Polarized on a Basic Strength

Thinking and risking are the two basic strengths within us that together create our existence as individuals. Each requires the other for its own creative fulfillment. Creative thinking requires risk and exposure. Creative risking requires reason and judgment. Neither can be creative without the other.

As we shift emphasis back and forth between thought and action, we sometimes get stuck in one or the other. As individuals, we tend to become stuck more easily on our lead strengths. Those who lead in thinking will more easily polarize on thinking than risking. Those who lead in risking will more easily polarize on risking than thinking. Since we can't solve our problems with either thinking or risking alone, becoming polarized on either one inevitably leads to failure.

In Figure 8, a spiral of decay is drawn in both the thinking and risking loops, giving a visual image of what happens when we become hung up in either loop. Below each loop, a series of statements describes how we think and behave when we polarize on each of the two strengths.

Six of the common tendencies listed in Figure 7 are identified as personal tendencies that can take us toward polarization on the thinking strength. They are listed below.

   2 . . avoid confrontation and conflict *when it's time to* express real thoughts and feelings.

   6 . . wait for the other person to make the first move *when it's time to* take the initiative.

# Becoming Polarized on a Basic Strength

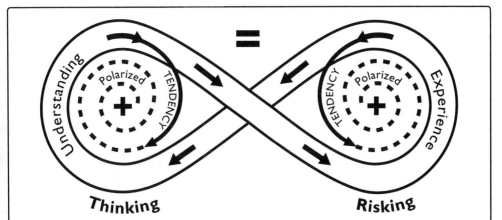

## Signs of Becoming Polarized on Thinking

Continues to think when it's time to get into action.

Build-up of ideas and plans.

Stability and order become increasingly important.

Takes fewer and fewer risks.

Holds feelings inside.

Resists change.

Holds on to established ways.

Procrastinates.

Feels more and more depressed and anxious.

Becomes more and more "removed" and "out of it."

**Immobilized.**

## Signs of Becoming Polarized on Risking

Continues to engage in action when it's time to stop and think.

Build-up of activity and movement.

Action becomes increasingly important.

Thinks less and less.

Expresses feelings aggressively.

Resists thoughtful analysis.

Quick to change things.

Makes quick decisions.

Feels increasingly exposed and agitated.

Becomes more and more emotional.

**Out of control.**

*Figure 8*

8 . . hold onto established ways *when it's time to* change and try new things.

13 . . hold feelings inside *when it's time to* express them openly.

23 . . be quiet and listen *when it's time to* speak out.

27 . . analyze the problem *when it's time to* take action.

There are also six common tendencies listed in Figure 6 that may take us toward polarization on the risking strength. They are:

1 . . talk *when it's time to* listen.

9 . . stay emotionally involved *when it's time to* back off and be more objective.

12 . . make the decision *when it's time to* think more before deciding.

19 . . change things *when it's time to* hold steady and keep things the way they are.

24 . . take risks *when it's time to* take fewer chances.

28 . . assertively express thoughts and feelings *when it's time to* be more reserved and quiet.

# Becoming Polarized on a Thinking Strength

We can become polarized on one of our basic strengths, and we can also become polarized on any one of the four individual strengths that come out of the two basic strengths. We can become stuck on one type of thinking, and we can also become stuck on one type of risking. In this section, we deal with polarization on one type of thinking.

What happens when we polarize on our practical thinking strength? Practical thinking deals with facts and reality. It enables

# Becoming Polarized on a Thinking Strength

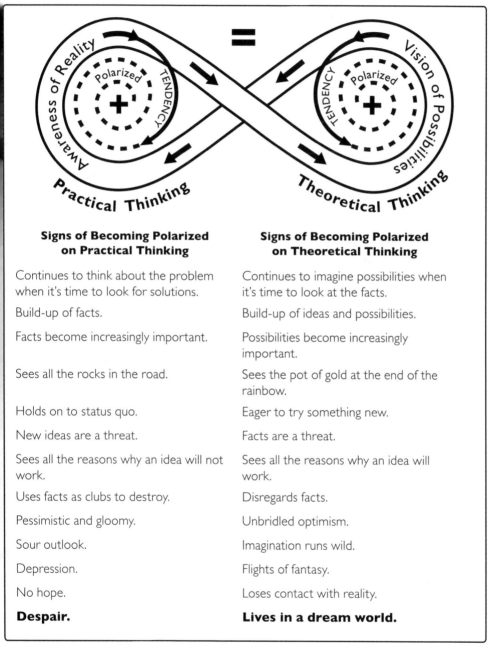

| **Signs of Becoming Polarized on Practical Thinking** | **Signs of Becoming Polarized on Theoretical Thinking** |
|---|---|
| Continues to think about the problem when it's time to look for solutions. | Continues to imagine possibilities when it's time to look at the facts. |
| Build-up of facts. | Build-up of ideas and possibilities. |
| Facts become increasingly important. | Possibilities become increasingly important. |
| Sees all the rocks in the road. | Sees the pot of gold at the end of the rainbow. |
| Holds on to status quo. | Eager to try something new. |
| New ideas are a threat. | Facts are a threat. |
| Sees all the reasons why an idea will not work. | Sees all the reasons why an idea will work. |
| Uses facts as clubs to destroy. | Disregards facts. |
| Pessimistic and gloomy. | Unbridled optimism. |
| Sour outlook. | Imagination runs wild. |
| Depression. | Flights of fantasy. |
| No hope. | Loses contact with reality. |
| **Despair.** | **Lives in a dream world.** |

*Figure 9*

us to see things as they are and identify real problems. Sometimes, we get hung up on identifying problems. Then it's like a broken record. We identify the problem, then we identify the problem, and then we identify the problem some more. It is way past time to start looking for solutions, and there we are still identifying the problem. The longer we stay stuck on the practical side, the more frustrated, unhappy, and nonproductive we become. In Figure 9, a spiral of decay is drawn in the practical thinking loop to give a visual image of what happens when we polarize on the practical side.

Also in Figure 9, there is a series of statements below the practical thinking loop. As you read down the page, the statements suggest increasing pain, frustration, and unhappiness. They describe how we feel and behave as polarization deepens. At the bottom, we use the terms "depression," "no hope," and "despair" to describe how we feel when we polarize deeply on the practical side. Most of us find some way to shift gears before we reach the point of despair, but we all experience some degree of pain and frustration before we make the shift. This is the way a normal person experiences life. If you have a tendency to emphasize practical thinking, it is very normal for you to hold onto the *status quo*, experience new ideas as a threat, and be tempted to depreciate and reject new ideas. Whether or not you experience depression, no hope, and despair depends upon how deeply you get mired in the practical side.

Now let's take a look at what happens when we polarize on our theoretical side. The process is the same as we just described for practical thinking. The difference is that now we are emphasizing theoretical possibilities and refusing to use our practical thinking abilities—we are stuck on the theoretical side. The broken record is playing a different tune now. We imagine possibilities, then we imagine possibilities, and then we imagine some more possibilities. The deepening process is indicated by both the spiral of decay in the theoretical loop and the sequence of statements under it. As we go down the right-hand side of the chart, the statements suggest more and more rejection of reality. At the bottom, we have the statement: "Lives in a dream world." Most of us make the shift to the practical side before we reach the lower levels. Those of us who tend to polarize on theoretical thinking, however, can usually identify strongly with the first few statements.

Listed below are some common tendencies from Figure 7 that can take us toward polarization on practical thinking:

11 . . think about problems *when it's time to* look for solutions.

20 . . emphasize the realities *when it's time to* emphasize the possibilities.

30 . . be practical and realistic *when it's time to* be more imaginative.

These tendencies can take us toward polarization on theoretical thinking:

5 . . imagine the possibilities *when it's time to* get the facts.

15 . . think about theory *when it's time to* be practical.

25 . . speculate about future possibilities *when it's time to* look at present realities.

# Becoming Polarized on a Risking Strength

When we use our strengths defensively, we can also become polarized on one type of risking. When we do, we disregard and depreciate the other type. This causes us to enter into a tightening spiral of decay that becomes increasingly painful—we get uptight. As polarization deepens, we become more defensive and less productive. We experience more and more frustration, unhappiness, and failure.

Figure 10 gives a visual picture of how we can polarize on either type of risking. Below each of the risking loops, a series of statements is listed. These statements describe what happens to us when we polarize. First, read down each of the two lists separately to get a feel for the progressive nature of the decay process. Next, go down the page a second time, reading the corresponding statements opposite each other on the two lists.

Six of the common tendencies listed in Figure 7 can take us toward polarization on dependent risking, and six others can take us toward polarization on independent risking. They are listed below.

Tendencies that can take us toward polarization on dependent risking are:

3... say "yes" *when it's time to* say "no."

10 .. go along with others *when it's time to* go your own way.

16 .. depend on others *when it's time to* depend on yourself.

18 .. be sympathetic and supportive *when it's time to* require others to be more responsible.

22 .. do things that please others *when it's time to* pay more attention to own needs and desires.

29 .. be tolerant of others *when it's time to* be more firm with others.

Tendencies that can take us toward polarization on independent risking are:

4 .. withdraw into own self-sufficiency *when it's time to* draw on the strengths of others.

7 .. compete with others *when it's time to* be cooperative.

# Becoming Polarized on a Risking Strength

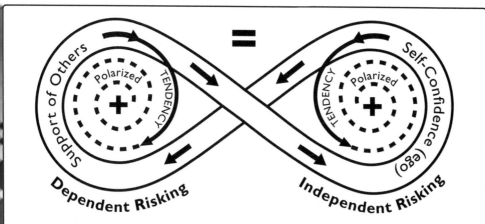

| **Signs of Becoming Polarized on Dependent Risking** | **Signs of Becoming Polarized on Independent Risking** |
|---|---|
| Continues to depend on others when it's time to depend on self. | Continues to depend on self when it's time to depend on others. |
| Build-up of support and approval of others. | Build-up of ego and self-confidence. |
| Support and approval of others becomes increasingly important. | Personal power and freedom becomes increasingly important. |
| Fewer and fewer expressions of independence. | Fewer and fewer expressions of dependence. |
| Says "yes" when should say "no." | Talks when should be listening. |
| Becomes less and less responsible. | Assumes more and more responsibility. |
| Loses self-confidence. | Loses confidence in others. |
| Loses awareness of self. | Loses awareness of others. |
| Loses the respect of others. | Loses the support and approval of others. |
| **Finally, loses the support and approval of others, the very thing that is most dear.** | **Finally, loses personal power and freedom, the very thing that is most dear.** |

Figure 10

14 . . drive hard to accomplish own goals *when it's time to* find out what others are thinking and feeling.

17 . . do things personally *when it's time to* trust others to do them.

21 . . be impatient with others *when it's time to* be more understanding of others.

26 . . think own thoughts *when it's time to* listen to what others are saying.

In this chapter, we have described where negative and destructive forces come from and how we experience them in our lives. In the next chapter, we will discuss how we can respond to the problems and pains that are inherent in human life. Our approach will be to regard these pains as growth challenges and to describe ways in which we can blend our strengths to keep us in the growth process. Only in this way can we experience the rewards that come from being a part of the process that is creating our world.

# 9

# Personal Growth

The Power of Opposite Strengths is based on the assumption that it is natural for people to grow and develop their potential. We naturally participate in the growth process throughout our lifetime. Once we develop the requisite level of conscious awareness, we participate in the process *consciously*. Our conscious awareness gives us the power to make personal choices that tend to either keep us in or take us out of the growth process. The nature of these conscious personal choices is the focus of this chapter.

At the end of Chapter 6 (The Growth Process), three growth choices were identified:

1. the choice to be ourselves

2. the choice to be flexible and adapt to the needs of the situation

3. the choice to make the sacrifice that is inherent in doing both (1) and (2).

The human condition requires that we make a positive choice in all three cases in order to stay in the growth process. It is a forced choice situation—we make the positive choices required, or we find ourselves spiraling into polarization. There is no middle ground. With the emergence of human consciousness, human beings must either choose participation in the process or eventually experience the painful effects of psychological decay.

The eight patterns of strengths and the concepts on which they are based give us a conceptual system that may be used to be more specific about how we make these three growth choices. We can use the patterns as a more specific definition of our natural way of being and, from this foundation, be ourselves even more fully. We can also use the concept of flex-patterns to develop a better idea of how we can become more flexible in expressing our supporting strengths and still remain true to ourselves. Finally, we can use our awareness of our strengths and the values they give us as a means to identify more clearly what we need to sacrifice in order to stay in the growth process and, as a result, to grow as individuals.

# Being True to Ourselves

In the Power of Opposite Strengths, being true to oneself is equivalent to being true to one's pattern of strengths. That is the essence of a healthy relationship with oneself. We are true to our patterns when we express our natural blend of lead and supporting strengths. Our lead strengths are in the foreground, giving us a self-identify and a unique individuality. Our supporting strengths are in the background, giving us the flexibility to deal creatively with the outside world. Although our lead strengths are dominant, our supporting strengths are always there and contribute to making us whole people.

In being true to ourselves, we do what comes naturally and show the world who we are. We follow our natural way, in spite of outside pressures that may influence us to do otherwise. We follow our natural tendencies and stand ready to deal with the problems they may cause. We have no desire to be someone else, nor do we wish to change our basic nature.

When we are being ourselves, we seek opportunities to use our natural talents and do those things that we do best. We feel good about who we are and have a strong sense of self-worth. Our basic natural pattern flavors whatever we do. Although we may display a good deal of flexibility and gain considerable skill in expressing our supporting strengths, the identity of our basic pattern shows through.

# Being True to the Situation

We are true to the external situation when we emphasize the strength that is appropriate, regardless of our own pattern of strengths. Becoming effective in expressing the strength appropriate to the situation requires a ready willingness to express our supporting strengths. We use the concept of flex-patterns to show how we can shift emphasis to any of our three supporting strengths and still maintain a healthy and productive relationship with ourselves.

The concept of flex-patterns assumes that not only do we have a natural blend of opposite strengths (our basic natural pattern), but we also have the capacity to express a different blend of these strengths when it is appropriate to the situation. This capacity gives us flexibility in expressing our strengths and the ability to adapt and adjust to the demands of our environment. When we emphasize one of our supporting strengths, we express a changed blend of strengths and display the characteristics of a pattern that is different from our natural pattern. By emphasizing each of our three supporting strengths one at a time, we can express three different patterns that have two lead strengths in common with our basic natural pattern. These patterns are what we refer to as our three flex-patterns.

Since our flex-patterns are those that have two lead strengths in common with our natural pattern, they are the ones that are most similar to our natural pattern. In expressing a flex-pattern, we shift emphasis to one of our supporting strengths, while maintaining our natural leanings in the other two pairs. This permits us to be flexible and meet the need of the situation, while still expressing a strong flavoring of our natural pattern.

Being flexible and gaining skill in expressing our three flex-patterns at appropriate times are markers of personal maturity. As we become more adept in expressing our flex-patterns, we develop more effectiveness in dealing creatively with a variety of situations. However, there is a limit to our flexibility. Beyond this limit, we become so flexible and adaptable that we begin to lose ourselves and no longer remain true to our basic nature.

Our three flex-patterns are each only a single step removed from our natural pattern. In our flex-patterns, we have the same lead strength in two of the pairs, and we have the opposite lead strength in only one pair. This makes our flex-patterns relatively similar to our natural pattern and relatively easy for us to express.

There are three other patterns that are two steps removed from our natural pattern. These three patterns have opposite lead strengths in two of the pairs, and they have only one lead strength in common with our natural pattern. This makes these patterns considerably different from our natural pattern and, as a result, more difficult for us to express and still maintain our natural way. In order to show these patterns, we must shift emphasis to two supporting strengths at one time and still be true to ourselves. We tend to find this awkward, and, if we keep it up for a long period of time, we can begin to lose the vitality and productivity of our natural way. We tend toward becoming phony. We are certainly faced with situations that require an emphasis on two of our supporting strengths. We need to deal with these situations as creatively as we can, but we need to be aware of the difficulty we face in maintaining the integrity of our basic pattern and the risk we run in losing ourselves.

There is one pattern that is our pattern opposite, and expressing it requires us to emphasize all three of our supporting strengths at one time. The difficulty and risk we run in trying to express our opposite pattern are extreme. We may be able to do it for short periods of time, but trying to maintain such a mask of our true nature for any extended period will almost surely result in problems for us and the world around us. We rob the world of the finest contributions we have to make and deprive ourselves of the fulfilling experiences that accompany the expression of our natural pattern of strengths.

In personal growth, the ultimate goal is to be a full, contributing member in the growth process. We make our fullest contribution to the process when we value it more highly than anything else. With the process at the center of our awareness, we give it all that we have—our strengths and the fruits that our strengths produce. When we make the choices that benefit the process, we discover that we are growing as persons.

Personal growth is much like happiness. If we try to be happy, it never happens. When we are doing the right things and forget about trying to be happy, happiness comes to us. The same is true with personal growth. When we forget about trying to grow and go about using our strengths for the positive benefit of the creative process, then, as an afterthought, we look back and discover we have grown.

The growth process requires the fruits of our strengths. If we are to remain in the growth process, we must sacrifice the fruits of our strengths and let them be used up in the process. If we fail to make the positive choice to give up the fruits we have produced, we become polarized on them and enter a process of psychological decay. In this process, not only do we experience the increasing pain and anguish associated with deepening polarization, but we eventually lose the very fruit we sought to save. It decays into nothingness because it is no longer a part of the process.

Making the sacrifice is the really hard part of staying in the growth process, because it involves a free choice to give up something that has great value to us. In fact, the most important sacrifices we need to make are those involving the things that mean the most to us. The one thing we must *never* give up is our commitment to and involvement in the creative process. We need to hold fast to the process and sacrifice all we have to it.

The idea of sacrifice appears to go against the grain with most of us. It seems that we are forever trying to get something for nothing, and that the desire to avoid paying the price is part of being human. We all have tried to have our cake and eat it too. As normal, healthy people grow and mature, one of the lessons they tend to learn is that we do have to make sacrifices to live a worthwhile life. We learn that any pain we experience in making the sacrifice is temporary and is overshadowed by the rewards of participating in the process.

One point needs to be re-emphasized: Personal growth requires that we meet the demands of all three of the growth choices. When we are in the process, we:

1. are true to ourselves

2. express the strength that is appropriate to the situation

3. willingly sacrifice the fruits of our strengths.

Very mature people appear to do all three things well. First, their natural pattern of strengths is distinctive and unmistakable. Not only do their lead strengths show clearly, but their natural leanings also create problems for them. They are not perfect people who never make mistakes. Second, they are highly flexible. They shift quickly and skillfully to their supporting strengths when the situation requires it, and they do it without a hint of phoniness. When they express their flex-patterns, they do it in their own ways: the flavor of the natural pattern is still there. Third, very mature people are willing to go through the pain of sacrifice and pay the price that is an integral part of being in the process and living a creative life.

# Dealing Creatively With Our Personal Tendencies

Each of the eight patterns of strengths tends to produce particular personal tendencies. Although the different patterns produce different tendencies and growth challenges, having one pattern or the other does not make it easier or harder for us to grow. One pattern produces just as many growth challenges as another, and they are equally difficult—they are simply different challenges. We therefore have no basis for feeling fortunate or unfortunate about having a particular pattern of strengths. We can all rest assured that people who have natural patterns that are different from ours have just as much difficulty dealing with their growth challenges as we have dealing with our own.

Now it is time to be specific about the growth challenges that each pattern tends to produce and to discuss how we can respond to these challenges creatively in order to grow as individuals. We will do this by selecting a typical tendency for each of the eight patterns and discussing the growth choices we must make to deal creatively with that particular tendency.

| Lead Strengths | Supporting Strengths | Flex-patterns |
|---|---|---|
| Thinking | Risking | V |
| Practical thinking | Theoretical thinking | III |
| Dependent risking | Independent risking | II |

**Typical Tendency:** avoid confrontation and conflict *when it's time to* express real thoughts and feelings.

## Being True To Oneself

People with Pattern I strengths are naturally quiet, respectful, and accepting in their relationships. They are good listeners and tend to wait for the other person to make the first move. These are essential ingredients in both warm relationships and good communication. Their first growth choice is to express these strengths and follow their natural tendencies.

As those with Pattern I strengths follow their natural tendencies, before long they begin to experience problems. Sometimes they discover that others are taking advantage of their good natures. Others may disregard and ignore them. These depreciating attitudes from others tend to cause Pattern Is to feel bad about themselves. The pain of polarization has begun and will continue to deepen and stimulate even more intense negative feelings until more equality is brought to the relationship.

## Being Flexible

To solve the problem caused by their tendency to avoid confrontation and conflict, those with Pattern I strengths need to shift to their Flex-pattern II and express more independence. By making this shift, they maintain the force of their natural way in both thinking and practicality, consciously focusing their energies on blending more independence into their behavior.

Pattern Is need to plan their actions carefully so as to approach needed confrontations in a stable, organized way. The painful emotions they are experiencing will be obvious and will have a strong impact on the people they confront, but the expression of these emotions will be controlled by their thinking strength.

## Paying the Price

When those with Pattern I strengths express their own thoughts and feelings openly, what price must they be ready to pay? The most important is the stability and *status quo* of the relationship. The confrontation and conflict they initiate will change the relationship into a dynamic and emotional interaction.

They must also stand ready to sacrifice the support and approval of the people they are confronting. There is a distinct risk that a serious conflict will be generated, and the other person will withdraw support. Being prepared to give up this support will enhance a Patter I's ability to express independence in a more forceful way.

## Payoff

What is the payoff to people with Pattern I strengths when they effectively express their thoughts and feelings, even if it means the possibility of confrontation and conflict? The biggest payoff is an immediate increase in self-esteem and self-confidence. Another payoff is being relieved of the bottled-up hostilities that typically have built up over time and become a heavy burden. A final payoff is increased respect from other people.

What about the payoff for the other people in the relationship? Almost invariably, the other person feels good about the Pattern I having responded in an open way and having come on straight about his or her real feelings. The confrontation clears the air and provides a strong basis on which the two can build a deeper and more creative relationship in the future.

| Lead Strengths | Supporting Strengths | Flex-patterns |
|---|---|---|
| Thinking | Risking | VII |
| Practical thinking | Theoretical thinking | IV |
| Independent risking | Dependent risking | I |

**Typical Tendency:** hold feelings inside *when it's time to* express them openly.

## Being True to Oneself

People with Pattern II strengths are naturally calm and self-controlled in their relationships. Their objectivity and cool rationality bring stability and order to their interactions with other people. These are excellent strengths, and they contribute essential ingredients to a healthy, productive relationship between two people. The first growth choice for people who have these leanings is to go their natural way and bring rationality and stability to their relationships.

As people with Pattern II strengths follow their natural tendency to emphasize rationality and control over their feelings, before long their relationships begin to suffer due to a dearth of emotional expression. They begin to feel a need for closer and more satisfying relationships that only an expression of real feelings can bring about. Others, meanwhile, may feel rejected and shut out by them. This need for an expression of feelings and a show of genuine emotion sets the stage for the second growth choice.

## Being Flexible

The second growth choice involves a willingness to relinquish some of the tight control they are exercising over their feelings. This is done by shifting to their Flex-pattern VII and risking an expression of their feelings. Then they can maintain the force of their natural way by continuing to be practical and independent but, at the same time, engage in a more active expression of their real feelings.

To be most effective in expressing their feelings more openly, those with Pattern II strengths need to maintain a good deal of control over their feelings (which comes naturally), and at the same time, let their guards down a bit and tell the other parties how they are feeling. They need to loosen their tight grips on their feelings and let them bubble up to the surface so they are revealed in a semi-controlled way.

## Paying the Price
What price must those with Pattern II strengths be ready to pay when they express their feelings? It is the loss of control over their own feelings and over the relationship itself. When the intensity of the Pattern II's feelings is brought out in the open, the relationship could become explosive and dynamic. Therefore, he or she must be willing to sacrifice a stable, somewhat distant relationship for the potential gain of developing a closer emotional relationship that could flower into a truly close friendship.

## Payoff
What is the payoff when people with Pattern II strengths risk expressing their real feelings in their natural way? First, it feels good to get one's feelings out in the open. It clears the air and relieves tension. Second, the other person in the relationship feels relieved, because now he or she knows where the Pattern II is coming from. Third, it creates a solid and honest basis on which to build a productive and satisfying relationship that deepens with time.

## PATTERN III

| Lead Strengths | Supporting Strengths | Flex-patterns |
|---|---|---|
| Thinking | Risking | VI |
| Theoretical thinking | Practical thinking | I |
| Dependent risking | Independent risking | IV |

**Typical tendency:** be quiet and listen *when it's time to* speak out.

# Being True to Oneself

People with Pattern III strengths are naturally quiet, respectful, and supportive in their relationships. They are mild-mannered and usually wait for others to take the initiative. They are thoughtful of others and are usually good listeners. When they follow their natural way, they bring stability, acceptance, and warmth to a relationship. Their first growth choice is to be true to themselves and bring these strengths to their relationships.

As they follow their natural, quiet way, before long they discover it is time for them to take the initiative and speak out. Their relationships begin to suffer because others may be taking them for granted or running over them. In any event, there always comes a time when their relationships demand that they speak out and let others know what they are thinking and how they are feeling. This need to speak out presents them with their second growth choice.

# Being Flexible

In speaking out, those with Pattern III strengths must emphasize their risking strength by shifting to their Flex-pattern VI. They still maintain their natural warmth, but they become more active in expressing their thoughts and real feelings. In doing this, they display many of the characteristics associated with the Pattern VI combination of strengths. They are deliberately more outgoing, active, and expressive. They get more involved and display more feeling and emotion.

## Paying the Price

What gives those with Pattern III strengths the courage to risk speaking out? It is the willingness to sacrifice the comfort and protection they receive by being quiet and not being noticed. If they speak out, they draw attention to themselves and lose their protective cover. A willingness to let go of this protective cover gives them the courage to expose themselves by speaking out.

## Payoff

What is the payoff if Pattern III people screw up their courage and speak out when the situation requires it? The first payoff is a feeling of involvement and a sense of aliveness. Life becomes more interesting and dynamic. Second, there is an enhanced feeling of closeness with other people and an increase in personal impact and self-esteem. The big payoff is in their relationships. With the introduction of stronger emotional elements, their relationships become much more dynamic and emotionally satisfying.

## PATTERN IV

| Lead Strengths | Supporting Strengths | Flex-patterns |
|---|---|---|
| Thinking | Risking | VIII |
| Theoretical thinking | Practical thinking | II |
| Independent risking | Dependent risking | III |

**Typical Tendency:** withdraw into own self-sufficiency *when it's time to* draw on the strength of others.

## Being True to Oneself

People with Pattern IV strengths tend to feel self-sufficient and able to take care of themselves. They tend to be strongly independent and go their own way. They have strong internal convictions and tend to feel a good deal of confidence in their ability to figure things out on their own. They usually make their greatest contributions by coming up with new and innovative ideas.

The first growth choice for those with Pattern IV strengths is to be themselves by relying on their own strengths to develop new approaches to solving old problems. As they follow their natural inclination to work alone and rely on their own strengths, they develop a need to interact with and draw on the strengths of other people. The emergence of this need to be dependent on others is what creates their second growth choice. Now they must make a conscious choice between continuing their natural self-sufficiency and depending more upon others.

## Being Flexible

When those with Pattern IV strengths deliberately shift emphasis to their supporting strength in dependent risking, they show many of the characteristics of their Flex-pattern III. Although there is still a strong flavor of independence and self-confidence, they become warmer and more accepting, more understanding and supportive of others. They listen more carefully to others and try to understand their points of view. They develop more patience and build stronger ties with others. They participate more fully in the strength of the group. By shifting to their Flex-pattern III, those with Pattern IV strengths still emphasize two of their lead strengths (thinking and theoretical thinking) and make the shift to dependent risking. The result is a strong flavoring of their Pattern IV nature but with more awareness of and concern for others.

## Paying the Price

What must those with Pattern IV strengths sacrifice when they deliberately emphasize their dependent risking? One of the most important values they must give up is their own self-importance. Now they must use their self-confidence to run the risk of depending more on others. They must put their own ideas out on the table and let them be criticized and judged by others. If they are willing to turn loose of their ideas, the sacrifice will give them the courage to depend on and listen to other people.

## Payoff

What is the payoff for those with Pattern IV strengths when they let go of some of their ego and depend more on the strengths of others? One of the greatest benefits is that they receive more data and information from others. This information gives them more raw materials to use in developing even better ideas. Another benefit is on the emotional level. As they interact more with others and make themselves more vulnerable through depending on other people, they feel and actually receive more support and approval from others. This gives them a stronger base of confidence. They still retain their basic thrust as innovators of fresh ideas, but they have more information to deal with and more courage to let their ideas be tested by reality.

### Pattern V

| Lead Strengths | Supporting Strengths | Flex-patterns |
|---|---|---|
| Risking | Thinking | I |
| Practical thinking | Theoretical thinking | VI |
| Dependent risking | Independent risking | VII |

**Typical Tendency:** say "yes" *when it's time to* say "no."

## Being True to Oneself

People who have the Pattern V combination of strengths are naturally outgoing, friendly, and supportive of other people. They tend to feel warm toward others and are inclined to help others. Although we all want the support and approval of others, those with Pattern V strengths have a particularly strong need to be well liked and recognized by others. They want to please others, and they frequently find themselves saying "yes" when really they should say "no." They can find they are so intent on pleasing others that the demands of others are running their lives.

Those with Pattern V strengths need to be true to their natural way and express their warm relationship strengths. They need to keep these natural strengths working in their relationships, even when they discover that these strengths have created a problem. To solve the problem, they need to blend in some of their supporting strengths, but they must keep the flavor of their natural way even while emphasizing a supporting strength.

## Being Flexible

When people with Pattern V strengths find that saying "yes" when they should say "no" is causing problems, they need to shift to their Flex-pattern VII and emphasize their independent risking strength. In doing this, they tend to show many of the characteristics associated with Pattern VII. They become more self-directed and show more independence in their relationship. They relate to others on a more nearly equal basis and bring their own needs into the equation more forcefully. They learn to say "no" in a nice way, but to do it with firmness. Their natural acceptance and warmth toward the other person gives a background flavor to their interactions, but the deliberate expression of their independence introduces a self-interest that needs to be taken into account.

## Paying the Price

What price must Pattern V people pay when they deliberately emphasize their independent strength? By far the most important sacrifice that may be required is the loss of the support and approval of others. When they express independence by saying "no," they run the distinct risk of losing the support of the other person. When they are able to consciously let go of this support and give it up to the process, they gain the courage to go ahead and express the independence that is required for them to say "no."

## Payoff

In most instances, the biggest payoff from dealing creatively with this tendency is an immediate experience of freedom— the freedom to be oneself and to look after one's own interest. Other benefits include more self-respect, enhanced feelings of self-worth, and more self-confidence. The increase in self-esteem allows them to relate to others on a more objective basis with a stronger sense of equality. This personal growth provides the basis for healthier and even stronger relationships with other people.

| PATTERN **VI** | | |
|---|---|---|
| **Lead Strengths** | **Supporting Strengths** | **Flex-patterns** |
| Risking | Thinking | III |
| Theoretical thinking | Practical thinking | V |
| Dependent risking | Independent risking | VIII |

**Typical Tendency:** stay emotionally involved *when it's time to* back off and be more objective.

## Being True to Oneself

People with Pattern VI strengths are naturally active and outgoing. They are caring people who want to get involved with others. They are more oriented to feelings than facts. They live in a world of people and enjoy being close and intimate with others. They identify strongly with others and feel a great deal of compassion toward them.

Those who have these valuable relationship strengths need to express them and be true to their natural way. This is their first growth choice. As with all normal and healthy people, those with Pattern VI strengths also find that following their natural way will eventually create a problem. Sometimes they find they have become so close and involved with others that they are causing a problem for themselves and perhaps even for the other person. It is then time for them to back off and be more objective. This type of problem presents the second growth choice for them.

## Being Flexible

When those with Pattern VI strengths become aware that being so close and intimate is causing a problem, it is time for them to emphasize their thinking strength by shifting to their Flex-pattern III. They need to back off, take time to think about the situation, and develop a better rational understanding of what is going on.

When they shift to their Flex-pattern III, they become quieter and more reflective. They are more reserved in their relationships and don't come on so strong. Their natural leaning toward warmth and compassion is in the background, flavoring their actions, but they are more thoughtful and wait longer for the other person to respond on his or her own initiative.

## Paying the Price

What must those with Pattern VI strengths sacrifice in order to bring more objectivity and healthy distance into their relationships? They must be willing to give up some of the warm emotional feelings they experience in close, intimate relationships with other people. They must stand ready to sacrifice these warm feelings to the process and bring more objectivity, rationality, and respect for individuality into their relationships. Being convinced that healthy relationships include separation and independence as well as closeness and intimacy helps them to make this sacrifice.

## Payoff

What is the payoff when people with Pattern VI strengths bring more objectivity and distance into their relationship? The first comes to them personally. No longer do they feel burdened by problems that can be solved only by the other person. The second payoff comes to the other person in the relationship. No longer does he or she feel invaded and smothered by so much closeness. These two results help to strengthen the relationship and make it healthier and more productive for both parties.

## PATTERN VII

| Lead Strengths | Supporting Strengths | Flex-patterns |
|---|---|---|
| Risking | Thinking | II |
| Practical thinking | Theoretical thinking | VIII |
| Independent risking | Dependent risking | V |

**Typical Tendency:** be impatient with others *when it's time to* be more understanding of others.

## Being True to Oneself

Those with Pattern VII strengths are naturally self-assertive and goal-oriented. They are competitive, ambitious, and experience a good deal of self-confidence. They take the initiative and are action-oriented. They are doers and out-front leaders. These are all positive strengths and contribute to the creative process. The first growth choice for those with Pattern VII strengths is to be true to themselves and express their natural leadership strengths.

Pattern VIIs naturally feel a high drive to accomplish their goals, which tends to cause them to feel a good deal of impatience with any delay. It is therefore natural for people with this combination of strengths to display impatience and, as a result, to experience the problems that impatience can bring about. When they become aware of these problems, they are faced with their second growth choice—to deliberately express the supporting strengths that will solve the problems being caused by their impatience.

## Being Flexible

Impatience has its most destructive effects on one's relationships with other people. As those with Pattern VII strengths express their impatience, others tend to develop negative attitudes and feelings toward them. The usual result is that Pattern VIIs find it even more difficult to accomplish their goals, because others are fighting them rather than trying to help. To solve this problem, they need to shift to their Flex-pattern V and emphasize dependent risking. They need to shift their attention away from their own personal goals and pay more attention to the other person in the relationship. This concentrates their attention on the other person, and they can then better understand the other person's thoughts and feelings. They need to ask questions and listen rather than talk and give orders.

## Paying the Price

What must those with Pattern VII strengths sacrifice if they are to deal effectively with their impatience? They must sacrifice immediate self-gratification in accomplishing their personal goals and ambitions. They must give up taking immediate action and take time to plan a course of action that gives due consideration to the needs and desires of the other person in the relationship.

## Payoff

What is the payoff when Pattern VIIs learn to deal creatively with their natural impatience? Probably the most important is an increase in personal productivity and effectiveness. By maintaining their natural drive and intensity to accomplish while expressing more dependence on others, they become highly effective leaders with increased personal impact and influence on the world around them. A second benefit is the good relationships they create with other people. By expressing their dependence on others, they experience more support and approval from others, and others become more loyal to them.

## PATTERN VIII

| Lead Strengths | Supporting Strengths | Flex-patterns |
|---|---|---|
| Risking | Thinking | IV |
| Theoretical thinking | Practical thinking | VII |
| Independent risking | Dependent risking | VI |

**Typical Tendency:** talk *when it's time to* listen.

# Being True to Oneself

Those with Pattern VIII strengths are highly dynamic. They naturally seek to have a strong influence on other people. They are natural promoters who can capture a vision and sell it to others. They are exciting, enthusiastic, and persuasive. They initiate action and stimulate change.

Their first growth choice is to express these dynamic strengths and influence other people. In the process of being themselves, it is natural for them to be in the spotlight and do a lot of talking. Their second growth choice comes when they become aware that their talking is causing a problem, and the time arrives when they need to do less talking and more listening.

# Being Flexible

What strengths are Pattern VIIIs emphasizing when they talk less and listen more? The first shift they make is to their thinking strength. When they do this, they show the characteristics of their Flex-pattern IV. They are more thoughtful and concentrate on trying to understand the situation. The second shift is to their courage of dependence. In making the shift to dependence, they express their Flex-pattern VI. They pay more attention to the other person and try to put themselves in the other person's shoes.

## Paying the Price

What enables those with Pattern VIII strengths to deliberately stop talking so much and begin to listen more? It is giving up their personal impact—something that they value very highly. If they can let go of their egos and forego the experience of influencing others, they can easily shift into more reserved behavior and let themselves be influenced more strongly by other people.

## Payoff

What is the payoff when Pattern VIIIs learn to deal creatively with their tendency to talk when it is time for them to listen? The most important payoff is that they enhance their positive influence on others. When they talk less, other people pay more attention to what they have to say. Another benefit is that they learn more and develop a deeper understanding of what is going on in their relationships with other people. These two benefits combine to produce even better relationships with others.

# Sustained Success

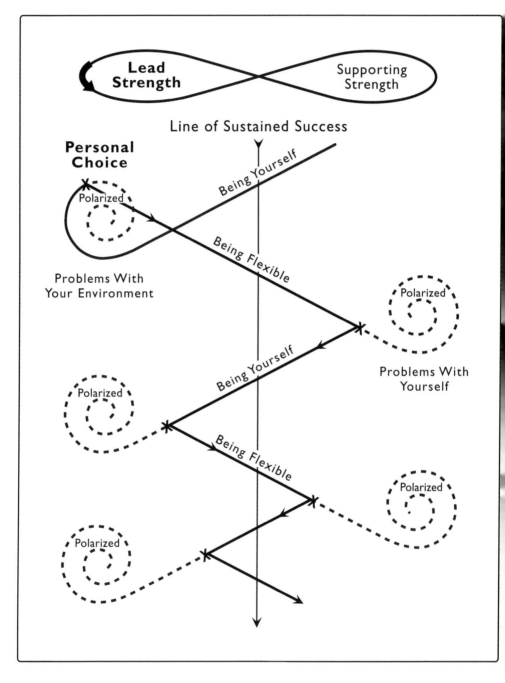

*Figure 11*

# Summary

This chapter has presented the model of personal growth that we have developed in the Power of Opposite Strengths. The diagram in Figure 11 summarizes the essential elements.

In Figure 11, the arrow appearing on the left end of the infinity symbol at the top represents the principle that every person has a lead strength and a supporting strength in each of the three pairs of opposite strengths. It also shows that we are naturally out-of-balance, in that we favor one of the strengths in a pair of opposite strengths.

The vertical line labeled "Line of Sustained Success" represents two things. The first is perfection—a perfect balance between the two opposite strengths. If one could travel straight down the Line of Sustained Success, one would always be perfectly balanced between the two opposite strengths. The second thing the vertical line represents is a speed bump. As we cross the line, we realize that it is time to slow down and become aware that if we continue our direction too long, we will become polarized. *One of the key understandings of how to grow personally and be successful is that the more often you cross the Line of Sustained Success, the more mature and effective you will become.*

We never go straight down this line. Instead, we always veer to one side or the other. This is in keeping with the fact that mature people don't seek perfection or perfect balance within themselves. Rather, they seek to contribute their natural talents and deal creatively with the problems that come their way. They recognize that their natural way takes them off to one side of perfection but affirm this as a part of the creative process at work in the world. A healthy relationship with oneself has at its core an acceptance and appreciation of one's natural pattern of strengths.

The painful choice at the "X" in the polarization spirals represents the place where we finally and reluctantly sacrifice the products of our strengths and feed them into the creative process. Making the choice at the "X" closer to the Line of Sustained Success indicates a much easier and more pleasant decision.

Mature people express their psychological health by doing two things well. First, they show their natural bias toward their lead strengths. In other words, they show who they are as real, out-of-balance human beings. They freely express their natural patterns. Second, they adapt quickly to problems by deliberately emphasizing their supporting strengths. In other words, they display flexibility by consciously emphasizing their supporting strengths when a situation requires it.

Creative and effective people do both of these things and avoid becoming polarized on either one. The flavor of the natural pattern is there and showing itself, yet, at the same time, they display flexibility by expressing their supporting strengths when appropriate. Through experience, they become more sensitive to the problems caused by going too far either way. On one hand, they become more aware of the problems caused by expressing their natural way of being and disregarding the needs of the situation. On the other hand, they become more aware of the problems caused when they become so flexible that they disregard their own natural way of being. In the first instance, they lose effectiveness in dealing with the real world. In the second instance, they tend to lose themselves. Both are painful experiences that call for a creative response.

The creative response is a painful choice to change directions and move to the opposite side. Through practice, people gain skill in making the appropriate shift at an earlier time and with more effectiveness. As they learn and grow, they spend more time close to their personal Line of Sustained Success and less time polarized on one side.

# Applying Opposite Strengths in Your Life

---

*Return to the Web site (**www.oppositestrengths.com**) to get your personalized **Guide to Being Flexible**.*

---

At the end of Part I, you generated your *Guide to Being Yourself* from your Member Home Page on *www.oppositestrengths.com*. Now it's time to generate the next Guide in the series—the *Guide to Being Flexible*. You can now add to your understanding of the experience of the executive coaching you are receiving or your experience of Part II of the Opposite Strengths Seminar—*Being Flexible*.

If you'd like, you can now have additional Other-report *Inventories* completed on you. Here again are the instructions for requesting Other-report *Inventories*.

- Go to our Web site, *www.oppositestrengths.com*, and log on by entering your Member ID and Member Password.
  My Member ID:
  My Member Password:

- After you log on, you will be taken to your personal Member Home Page. To have additional Other-report Inventories completed on you, look under the heading "Opposite Strengths Inventories," and click on the link "Ask someone to complete an Inventory on me." Then follow the instructions to request more Other-report *Inventories*.

- Now go to the upper left corner of your Member Home Page. You will see a heading entitled "Opposite Strengths Guides." Click on "Guide to Being Flexible." Your custom

*Guide to Being Flexible* will pop up in a separate window. There is both a Preview (short version) and Full Report (long version).

At the end of Part III of this book, I'll introduce you to the next online *Guide* available to you—the *Relationship Guide*. In order to generate this Guide, you must choose someone else who is going through Opposite Strengths Executive Coaching or an Opposite Strengths Seminar. If your entire organization is undergoing an Opposite Strengths Culture Transformation, you'll find lots of people you work with that you can create a *Relationship Guide* with. But don't do that now. First use your Opposite Strengths Executive Coaching or Opposite Strengths Seminar experience to get a clear understanding of how you can most easily be flexible – through your three flex-patterns – through the online *Guide to Being Flexible* you just generated from our Web site. Then you'll be ready to learn about how to apply what you've learned about your natural pattern of strengths (being yourself) and your three flex-patterns (being flexible) to establish and sustain successful relationships with everyone you know.

Now, please read on!

—Dr. Tommy Thomas

# Transition

Parts I and II of this book have dealt with understanding yourself and the growth process that allows you to be flexible—the essential aspects of your relationship with yourself. Now we will turn our attention to your relationships with other people.

Part III is about understanding other people and the relationship dynamics between people. It describes what is going on in a creative relationship between two people, discusses four distinct relationship tendencies that human beings experience, identifies the relationship characteristics each pattern tends to produce, and gives general guidance on strengthening relationships with others. We'll also show you how to generate your own *Relationship Guides* from our Web site.

# PART III
## Sustained Success in Relationships

# 10

# Dynamics of a Creative Relationship

Relationships with other people are a precious—and at times vexing—part of human life and society. Some of the most useful insights in the Power of Opposite Strengths concern our one-to-one relationships with others—with our spouses, children, business partners, employees, colleagues, friends, and others significant in our lives.

In this part of the book, the first three chapters will help you to understand other people. The first chapter lays the foundation for understanding one-to-one relationships by discussing the dynamics of a creative relationship. The second chapter describes the four fundamental relationship tendencies that people experience and express. The third chapter describes the relationship characteristics that each of the eight patterns of strengths tends to produce. The fourth chapter gives you general insights on how to strengthen your relationships.

## Relationship Dynamics

What are the dynamics of a creative and productive relationship between two people? What is actually going on when two people have good communication and a strong relationship? The purpose of this section is to answer these questions.

The straightforward answer is to say there are three basic dynamics that make a relationship creative. All are essential, and each one makes its own contribution to the creativeness of the relationship. The two people

- have an attitude of equality toward each other

- take the initiative to move toward each other

- are respectful of each other's territories.

In an effort to define the nature of these three dynamics more fully, it may be helpful to diagram how they would be manifested in a perfect relationship. Of course, a perfect relationship never

## A Creative Relationship

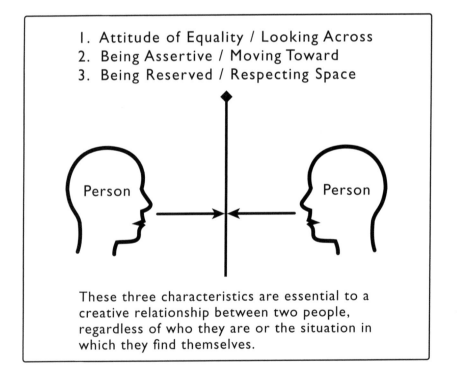

1. Attitude of Equality / Looking Across
2. Being Assertive / Moving Toward
3. Being Reserved / Respecting Space

Person                                    Person

These three characteristics are essential to a creative relationship between two people, regardless of who they are or the situation in which they find themselves.

*Figure 12*

exists between two real people. Even so, the concept of a perfect relationship may help us understand what is going on in our real relationships and see more clearly what we can do to strengthen them.

Figure 12 depicts a perfect relationship. The arrows coming from each person and meeting at the vertical line between them may be used to describe the three dynamics in a perfect relationship.

First, the horizontal positioning of the arrows suggests a level relationship—the two people look straight across at each other. They value themselves and each other on an equal basis. There is no looking up to or looking down upon going on in the relationship. This *attitude of equality* is an essential dynamic in a perfect relationship.

Second, the arrows going up to the line suggest that each person faces and approaches the other. There is a movement toward the other—an effort to make contact and enter into a relationship. This kind of assertion is required not only to make contact, but also to maintain and strengthen an ongoing relationship. *Being assertive and moving toward the other person* is the second dynamic in a perfect relationship.

Third, the fact that the arrows stop at the vertical line between the two people suggests that each person refrains from going over into the territory of the other. They respect each other's space, and each is careful not to go across the line and violate the rights of the other person. *Being respectful of the other person's territory* is the third dynamic in a perfect relationship.

Although we can never achieve a perfect relationship with another person, we do approximate it when we have a close friend. We have asked many people what a close friend means to them. Although people respond differently and tend to emphasize one of the dynamics discussed above, the thread of each of the three dynamics usually appears in some form. Many people describe a close-friend relationship as one in which they feel comfortable. They can be themselves and still be accepted. They do not have to be on guard because they know the other person will not take advantage of them. The idea of mutual concern is usually there, also. Many people say, "A close friend is someone I would help if needed and someone I know would help me if I needed it." The word "trust" is frequently used: "A close friend is someone I can trust—someone I can confide in and know it won't go any farther."

Guidelines for living together in society that have stood the test of time seem to combine these three characteristics in some way. The Judeo-Christian heritage of Western civilization gives us two excellent examples in the sayings, "Love your neighbor as yourself," and "Do unto others as you would have them do unto you." They suggest equality as well as a balance between self-assertion and respect for the other person.

In summary, there are three dynamics in a perfect relationship. First, the two people are looking straight across at each other, affirming their own worth and the worth of the other person on an equal basis. Second, both are being assertive and moving toward the other person, seeking to establish and deepen the relationship. Third, both are respectful of the other person's space and careful not to go across the line into the other's rightful territory.

## The Line of Sustained Success

In Figure 12, the vertical line drawn between the two people is referred to as the "Line of Sustained Success." In a perfect relationship, it represents the point up to which each person goes, and stops, when both are expressing a perfect balance between assertiveness and reserved behavior. Meeting at the Line of Sustained Success represents the most creative, productive, and mutually satisfying relationship two people can have.

In a perfect relationship, the vertical line between the two people is drawn in the middle, suggesting that we are dealing with two hypothetical people who are always in the same situation. In other words, neither the individual differences of any two actual people nor the changing situation in which real people would live are taken into account.

In our real-life relationships, the only thing equal is our worth as individuals. In all other comparisons, we are unequal. We have different patterns of strengths, different amounts of strength, different levels of maturity, different degrees of authority, and different sets of tendencies. In addition to these individual differences, the situation in which two people find themselves is continually changing. Because of these natural differences between two real people and the changing situation in which they live, the Line of Sustained Success is never in the middle. It is closer to one side than the other, depending upon who the two people are and the situation in which they find themselves.

For example, in the relationship between a father and son, the father is normally more mature and has more strength and authority. A diagram of their relationship could be drawn as shown in Figure 13a. The Line of Sustained Success, being closer to the son, suggests that their most creative, productive, and satisfying relationship is one in which the father exerts more power and has more authority and freedom. Although they have equal worth as individuals and both look straight across at each other (suggested by the two horizontal arrows), the father is the dominant figure in the relationship. When the son grows up and is taking care of his aged father, their relationship might be diagrammed as shown in Figure 13b. They still have equal worth

# Two Father-Son Relationships

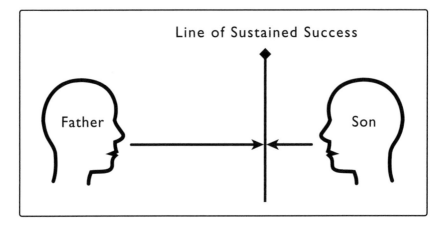

*Figure 13a*

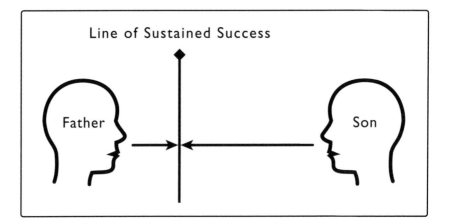

*Figure 13b*

## Supervisor-Subordinate Relationships

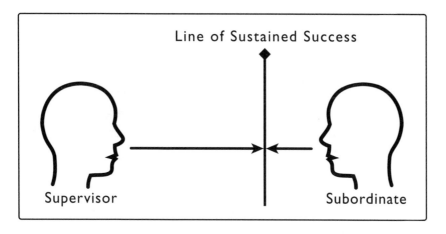

Figure 14

as individuals, but the son is now the stronger one and has the dominant influence in the relationship.

When two people are working together in a team effort, their individual contributions to the accomplishment of a common objective are never equal. One person is always contributing more than is the other. These differences can find expression in the corporate structure of an organization. In Figure 14, where the Line of Sustained Success is closer to the subordinate, the diagram shows that the supervisor has more power, freedom, and authority than the subordinate does. They still look straight across at each other and have equal worth as individuals, but the relative amounts of power, freedom, and authority that they enjoy determine the position of the Line of Sustained Success between them.

# The Zone of Sustained Success

In our real relationships, we don't come up to the Line of Sustained Success and stop. In the first place, we don't even know where the line is until we experiment some in the relationship. Perhaps at first we go too far across the line and then don't go far enough. In the second place, none of us is capable of relating that perfectly to another human being. We actually relate to another person in a *zone* of sustained success rather than on a Line of Sustained Success.

Figure 15 illustrates how two people actually relate to each other when they have a productive relationship. Each one is continually undershooting and overshooting the Line of Sustained Success. As the relationship becomes stronger and more creative, the zone of sustained success narrows. The zone never narrows

## Zone of Sustained Success

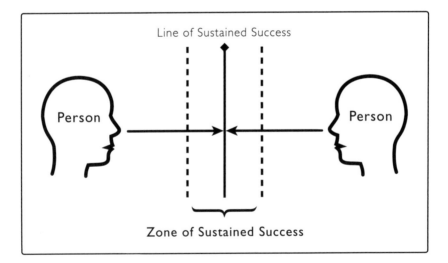

*Figure 15*

to a line, however. That would represent a state of perfection that real people are not equipped to reach. The Line of Sustained Success can be a goal toward which we strive, but it is not something we expect to achieve in reality.

Another useful concept in further defining the zone of sustained success is considering its upper and lower bounds in addition to the bounds on the side. The upper and lower bounds indicate that each person has some latitude in expressing dependent risking and independent risking in the relationship.

Visually, the zone of sustained success can be thought of as an ever-changing rectangle with its center point exactly midway between two people. This center point is the magical place in which they see eye-to-eye and value one another as equals. The zone of sustained success is the area around this center point in which they approximate a perfect relationship.

Each relationship is unique in its definition of the zone of sustained success. The remainder of this book is devoted to helping you find your own personal zones of sustained success with the people whose relationships are valuable to you.

# 11

# Relationship Tendencies

Human beings experience and express four distinct kinds of tendencies in their relationships with one another. These four tendencies are

- reserved and relational tendency
- reserved and independent tendency
- assertive and relational tendency
- assertive and independent tendency.

All four of these tendencies are expressions of positive, constructive strengths. Each makes its own contribution to a productive and satisfying relationship between two people.

These four tendencies are normal and natural forces that help shape every human relationship. As individuals, it is natural and normal for us to express some more frequently than others. When we consistently express one of these tendencies more frequently than the others, it becomes a distinguishing feature of our personality.

It is important for us to realize that our own inclination to express one of these tendencies more than the others is completely normal and natural. The intent here is not to encourage people to get rid of their tendencies, but rather to help them become aware of their tendencies and develop skill in dealing creatively with them when they cause problems. We assume that having such tendencies is a natural part of being a healthy and creative person, and that expressing them is a natural aspect of each person's individuality. With experience, we become aware of the problems they can cause us and, out of this awareness, we develop skill in dealing with them creatively.

When the Power of Opposite Strengths is used as an aid in strengthening our relationships, a good understanding of the four basic tendencies is essential. Because of the importance of this understanding, each tendency is discussed in some detail below. Diagrams illustrating how these tendencies are expressed in our relationships and how we are likely to be perceived when we express them are presented in Figure 16.

# Reserved and Relational Tendency

Two important strengths stand behind the reserved and relational tendency: the thinking strength and the dependent risking strength. These two strengths combine to provide stability and warmth in a relationship. The thinking strength brings a quiet reserve characterized by thoughtfulness, understanding, and respect. The dependent strength lends a warm glow to the relationship that is expressed in quiet appreciation, devotion, and loyalty.

The reserved and relational tendency is expressed in quiet, watchful-waiting behavior. An expression of this tendency is more of a reaction to what the other person does than a self-generated action. Behavior expressing this tendency is mild-mannered, reserved, cautious, tentative, and respectful.

Persons with Patterns I and III tend to experience and express the reserved and relational tendency most frequently (although people with all of the other patterns also can and do express this tendency at times).

The reserved and relational tendency is illustrated in the top section of Figure 16. The short, dropping arrow coming from the person (self) on the left represents the expression of the reserved and relational tendency. The reserved quality is represented by the arrow being drawn short of the Line of Sustained Success. It represents a hesitancy to be assertive and move toward the other person. The relational or dependent quality is represented by the dropping of the arrow, which suggests a tendency to depreciate oneself in the relationship.

Because the thinking and dependent strengths are emphasized in an expression of the reserved and relational tendency, the assertive and independent strengths are automatically de-emphasized. This relatively weak expression of assertiveness and independence can create an impression of personal weakness. As a result, others sometimes inaccurately and derogatorily describe those who express this tendency as weak, passive, indecisive, submissive, or timid. They may be unfairly discounted for giving in too easily, not standing up, lacking initiative, having no backbone, being afraid to speak up, etc. That said, if an individual is actually polarized on thinking and dependent risking, then terms like those take on more validity in describing the person's behavior.

In dealing creatively with this tendency, it is important for people to realize that the solution is neither to depreciate these strengths nor to refuse to express them. The creative solution lies in shifting emphasis to their opposite strengths. In this case, it would involve a shift to more assertiveness (risking) and more independence (independent risking). This is the flexing concept in action—the reserved and relational qualities are retained, but more assertiveness and independence are blended into the behavioral mix.

# Reserved and Independent Tendency

In the reserved and independent tendency, the thinking strength and the independent risking strength are emphasized. The expression of these two strengths gives the impression of intellectual competence and self-sufficiency. The thinking strength contributes rationality, stability, logic, and structure to the relationship. The independent strength provides leadership in defining and establishing objectives and provides the confidence, discipline, and determination needed to accomplish them.

The reserved quality in this tendency comes from an internal marshaling of strength to understand and solve a problem. Behavior expressing this tendency is usually characterized by intense concentration and detachment from the immediate surroundings. This intense mental activity gives an impression of strength and stability that can be likened to a whirling gyroscope: There is a great deal of activity within but practically no movement relative to the outside world. The independent quality comes from the emphasis on internal strengths—looking to resources within rather than outside. This orientation gives the impression of quiet self-confidence, self-sufficiency, self-directedness, and substantial internal strength.

People who frequently express this tendency are usually highly task-oriented, quality-minded, and dedicated to efficiency, and they show a good deal of bulldog tenacity. They feel comfortable being by themselves. They value their privacy.

Pattern IIs and Pattern IVs naturally tend to experience and express the reserved and independent tendency. Of course, people with other patterns may express this tendency because of what they have learned from their life experiences. In those instances, however, it is a learned tendency and not a natural or innate tendency.

The reserved and independent tendency is illustrated in the second section of Figure 16. The arrow coming out of the person (self) on the left represents the expression of the reserved and independent tendency. The reserved quality is represented by the arrow's abrupt change of direction, moving away from the other person. The upward movement of the arrow, suggesting self-confidence and self-sufficiency, represents the independent quality.

Because the thinking and independent strengths are emphasized in an expression of the reserved and independent tendency, the assertive and dependent strengths are automatically de-emphasized. This relatively weak expression of assertiveness and dependence causes people who express this tendency to be negatively and inaccurately described as cold, prudish, conceited, snobbish, priggish, uncaring, suspicious, distrustful, withdrawn, insensitive, stubborn, hardheaded, etc. However, if an individual becomes polarized on thinking and independent risking, such descriptions begin to describe the individual more accurately.

How do people deal creatively with the reserved and independent tendency when its expression is causing a problem? First, they must realize that they are expressing two good strengths—the thinking strength and independent risking strength. They should not feel the need to give up these strengths or even hold back from using them. Rather, they should make a conscious effort to express more of their own assertiveness (risking) and to risk more dependence (dependent risking). In terms of the flexing concept, those with a natural tendency toward being reserved and independent should continue to affirm and express their thinking and independence, but they should also consciously and deliberately blend in more of their assertive and dependent strengths. However, they should do this only after becoming aware that their natural tendency is causing a problem. If they try to police their reserved and independent tendency too closely, before it causes a problem, they tend to become something other than who they really are and lose the force and creativity of their natural lead strengths.

# Relationship Tendencies

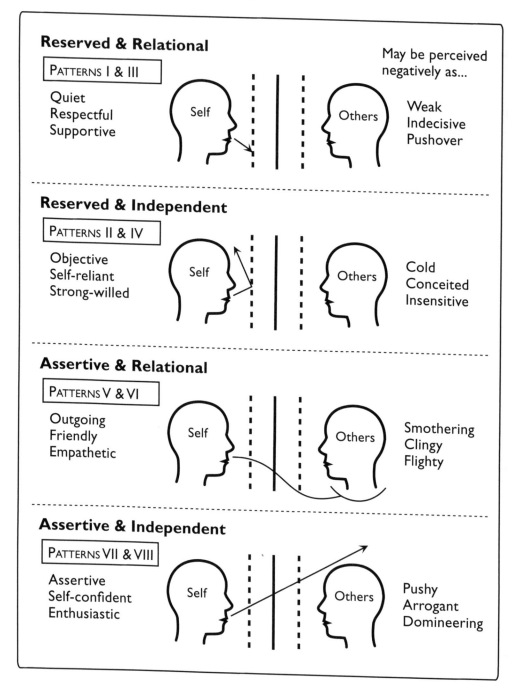

Figure 16

# Assertive and Relational Tendency

The assertive and relational tendency comes from emphasis on two important strengths: the dynamic, moving, risking strength, and the courageous, trusting, dependent risking strength. Together these two strengths bring a good deal of warmth and active caring to a relationship. People who express this tendency move toward others in an assertive way and seek to initiate contact and create a close relationship.

The assertive and relational tendency is expressed in active, reaching-out behavior that is characterized by friendliness and helpfulness. People with this tendency are supportive, sympathetic, and self-sacrificing. They center their attention on the other person rather than on themselves. They seek communication, sharing, and closeness. Usually they are highly social and emotionally expressive, and they feel at home dealing with feelings.

People with Patterns V and VI naturally tend to experience and express the assertive and relational tendency. Other patterns can express this tendency, of course, but for the Vs and VIs, it is a natural tendency that comes from their basic make-up.

The assertive and relational tendency is illustrated in the third section in Figure 16. The curved arrow coming out of the person (self) on the left and going across the Line of Sustained Success shows the assertive strength becoming an aggressive strength when it invades the territory of the other person. The downward, swooping arrow that ends up cradling the other person in active support shows that interest and concern tends to center on the other person.

Because the assertive and dependent strengths are emphasized in an expression of the assertive and relational tendency, the thinking strength and the independent risking strength are automatically de-emphasized. This relatively weak expression of thinking and independence sometimes causes people who express this tendency to be inaccurately described as clinging vines or copycats, or as being smothering, flighty, burdensome, mushy, emotionally unstable, sentimental, impressionable, too friendly, etc. If the individual is polarized on risking and dependent risking, however, negative descriptors like those above become more accurate.

Those who have a problem with the assertive and relational tendency can deal with it creatively by blending more thinking and more independence into their behavior. This requires a personal choice to shift emphasis to the thinking and independent risking strengths at appropriate times. The appropriate times are usually very specific and obvious, because those are the times when the tendency is causing the most problems.

Although a deliberate and conscious shift of emphasis to the thinking and independent strengths involves the risk of losing some of the fruits of action and warm dependence, it does not stop the activity of these strengths. Those who deal creatively with this tendency remain true to their natural way of being by keeping their natural assertiveness and dependence active in the background. Dealing effectively with a tendency does not involve changing one's basic nature.

# Assertive and Independent Tendency

Two important strengths are emphasized in the expression of the assertive and independent tendency: the dynamic, action-oriented risking strength, and the self-reliant independent risking strength. Together these two strengths stimulate enthusiasm, initiate action, and provide out-front leadership in a relationship.

In the expression of the assertive and independent tendency, the center of interest and concern is the self. Behavior expressing this tendency is characterized by self-confidence, self-awareness, and self-interest. Those who consistently express this tendency are self-starters, highly competitive, forceful, ambitious, and energetic. They drive hard to accomplish and usually have a strong impact on other people. They continually seek to expand their sphere of influence.

Pattern VIIs and VIIIs tend to experience and express the assertive and independent tendency most frequently. People with all patterns have the assertive and independent strengths available to them and emphasize these strengths at times, but VIIs and VIIIs have a natural tendency to lead with these strengths.

The bottom section in Figure 16 illustrates the assertive and independent tendency. The arrow coming out of the person (self) on the left represents the expression of the assertive and independent tendency. The portion of the arrow going across the Line of Sustained Success into the territory of the other person shows the aggressive element in the tendency—the tendency to invade the territory of the other person and establish dominion over it. The upward slant of the arrow suggests self-confidence.

In the expression of the assertive and independent tendency, the assertive, action-oriented strengths and the independent, self-oriented strengths are emphasized. This results in a de-emphasis on two other important strengths—thinking and dependent risking. Because of this, those who consistently express the assertive and independent tendency are sometimes described—both negatively and inaccurately—as bullies, braggarts, or loudmouths, or as pushy, domineering, impatient, egotistical, selfish, obnoxious, braggart, arrogant, presumptuous, combative, overbearing, or so forth. As was the case with the other tendencies, if the individual becomes polarized on the strengths being emphasized (in this case, risking and independent risking), then these negative terms begin to apply to the individual with more accuracy.

The assertive and independent tendency is dealt with most effectively and creatively by consciously and deliberately thinking more about the other person and expressing more dependence upon him or her. This involves centering one's attention on the other person, looking straight across to him or her as an equal, and asking questions and listening to what the other person has to say. When this is done creatively, the high internal drive to accomplish and the strong independent strength remain, but there is more awareness and concern for the other person, and more active dependence is placed upon the other person, as well. Just as with the other three tendencies, this shift of emphasis onto neglected strengths does not get rid of the assertive and independent tendency but brings balance and creativity to one's relationships.

# 12

# Relationship Characteristics of Each Pattern

This chapter describes the relationship characteristics that the eight patterns of strengths tend to produce. Each of the eight descriptions is presented separately.

### Pattern I

| Lead Strengths | Supporting Strengths | Flex-patterns |
|---|---|---|
| Thinking | Risking | V |
| Practical thinking | Theoretical thinking | III |
| Dependent risking | Independent risking | II |

## Relationship Strengths

People with Pattern I strengths normally bring a good deal of stability and warmth to a relationship. Their consistent and organized approach to the world can contribute much to a team effort, and their natural inclination toward cooperation makes them good team members. They are very dependable and can be counted on to keep things running smoothly on a consistent basis. Their natural warmth and concern for other people contributes to an atmosphere of acceptance and frequently pours oil on the troubled waters of a relationship. They are good listeners and are very supportive in their relationships. Loyalty is one of their finest strengths.

They can bring other values to their relationships by deliberately emphasizing their three supporting strengths. First, they can bring a spark of dynamism by emphasizing their risking strength (Flex-pattern V). Second, they can bring more conceptual understanding by emphasizing their theoretical thinking (Flex-pattern III). Third, they can bring stable leadership by emphasizing their independent strength (Flex-pattern II).

## Natural Tendencies

Normally, those with Pattern I strengths express the reserved and relational tendency more frequently than any other. They tend to be quiet, unassertive, supportive, and accepting in their relationships. The personal tendency that usually gives them the most trouble is avoiding confrontation and conflict by not expressing their thoughts and feelings. They tend to understate their needs and desires, and they feel uncomfortable standing up for their rights. Sometimes they are so quiet and respectful that other people don't know how they feel or what they want.

They have a natural urge to respond to the needs of others. Although this is an admirable and creative thing, when the urge is given free rein, they find that they are letting the needs and desires of others rule their lives. They no longer have time or energy for their own needs and desires.

Another tendency that frequently has an adverse effect on their relationships is to polarize on their problems and dwell on the negatives. When they fail to deal creatively with this tendency, they develop a negative attitude and become depressed. In turn, these negative feelings and attitudes can sour their relationships and drive people away from them.

## What Those with Pattern I
## Strengths Want From Others

People of all patterns want to be accepted and respected by others, but those who have Pattern I strengths usually experience this as an especially strong need. How others feel about them makes a great deal of difference in how they feel about themselves. They want recognition and encouragement, and they don't want to have to demand it from other people.

They also want to receive stimulation from others. They feel most comfortable when others are taking the initiative and causing things to happen, and they are being called on to help out. They want to be included and feel the support of other people.

They want to be needed by others, and they want others to help them feel good about themselves. They want others to take the leadership role, but they want to be recognized and appreciated for their own contributions.

### PATTERN II

| Lead Strengths | Supporting Strengths | Flex-patterns |
|---|---|---|
| Thinking | Risking | VII |
| Practical thinking | Theoretical thinking | IV |
| Independent risking | Dependent risking | I |

## Relationship Strengths

Those with Pattern II strengths bring stable leadership to their relationships—particularly through their rationality, practicality, and realistic planning. They take the initiative to organize and stabilize situations.

They also bring a sense of excellence to their relationships. They are quality-minded, and they set high standards for achievement. They provide objectivity, efficiency, discipline, and practical reasoning to a team effort.

Pattern IIs are self-confident and bring a solid feeling of power and confidence to their relationships. They provide motivation to see things through and stick with it when the going gets tough. They have a high internal drive for tangible accomplishment and give confidence to other people in a team effort.

People who have Pattern II strengths can bring other values to their relationships by deliberately emphasizing their three supporting strengths. First, they can stimulate more interaction and action by becoming more self-assertive (Flex-pattern VII). Second, they can bring an expanded awareness of possibilities by emphasizing their imaginative strengths (Flex-pattern IV). Third, they can bring more warmth and appreciation by emphasizing their dependent strengths (Flex-pattern I).

## Natural Tendencies

Those who have Pattern II strengths are naturally reserved and independent in their relationships. They are self-confident and have a tendency to withdraw into their own self-sufficiency. They are very much do-it-yourself people. Usually, it is a real chore for them to delegate authority and depend upon other people. Many who have this combination of strengths feel as if dependence on others is a weakness rather than a strength.

Pattern IIs have a tendency to be overly critical of other people. They tend to see other people's faults and shortcomings much more clearly than they see their potentials. Failure to deal creatively with this tendency can be very damaging to their relationships.

Perhaps the most frequently expressed tendency of people who have Pattern II strengths is that of holding their feelings within. Usually they find it very difficult to be emotionally expressive and show people their real feelings—particularly their warm, dependent feelings.

## What Those with Pattern II Strengths Want From Others

People with Pattern II strengths want space. Normally, they want other people to be objective and rational in the relationship. When they are aware the relationship needs an expression of warmth, they prefer the other person to take the initiative to express it. They want to be respected, and they particularly dislike other people trying to get too close. They want others to listen to them when they have something to say.

Those with Pattern II strengths prefer a relationship where the two people involved are working together to achieve a tangible result. They prefer a relationship that is task-oriented rather than relationship-oriented. They want others to be logical and rational and, above all, to make sense.

### PATTERN III

| Lead Strengths | Supporting Strengths | Flex-patterns |
| --- | --- | --- |
| Thinking | Risking | VI |
| Theoretical thinking | Practical thinking | I |
| Dependent risking | Independent risking | IV |

## Relationship Strengths

People who have Pattern III strengths contribute conceptual clarity to their relationships. They usually have a depth of understanding regarding ideas and theories—particularly those that are proven and well established. Usually they are an excellent source of information on a wide variety of subjects.

They bring approachability and quiet warmth to a relationship. They are supportive, agreeable, and tend to play the role of peacemaker. They can be a good communication link between two people who are having problems in their relationship.

Pattern IIIs are usually very conscientious. They bring stability, consistency, and dependability to their relationships. They tend to be respectful and thoughtful of others and are usually very sensitive to the feelings of others. They typically get along very well with other people and sometimes are cooperative to a fault.

Those who have the Pattern III combination of strengths can bring other values to their relationships by deliberately emphasizing their three supporting strengths. First, they can stimulate interaction that is more dynamic by emphasizing their assertive strengths (expressing their Flex-pattern VI). Second, they can bring more practicality and realism by emphasizing their practical thinking (expressing their Flex-pattern I). Third, they can bring more leadership to the relationship by emphasizing their independent strength (expressing their Flex-pattern IV).

## Natural Tendencies

People who have Pattern III strengths are naturally reserved and relational in their relationships. They tend to be unassertive and wait for others to make the first move. A number of those who have these strengths find their most troublesome tendency is to be quiet and not speak up when they should. Closely related to this tendency, they find it hard to say "no" and sometimes end up letting the demands and wishes of others rule their lives.

They tend to avoid confrontation and conflict if at all possible. Their tendency to exaggerate the importance of others and depreciate their own importance makes it difficult for them to stand up strongly for their own rights.

Another tendency they tend to experience is procrastination. This tendency to re-think a problem rather than commit themselves to a course of action is a common and recurring problem for most people who have this combination of strengths.

## What Those with Pattern III Strengths Want From Others

Pattern IIIs want to be appreciated and respected, without having to ask for it or demand it. They want others to help them feel good about themselves and give them encouragement.

Those who have Pattern III strengths like for others to take the initiative and provide dynamic stimulation. They are most comfortable when others take the leadership role and ask them for their help. They want to know they are needed and appreciated.

They want support and approval from other people. Although all patterns want this support and approval, with them it is a critical need. A good deal of their self-confidence comes from the support and approval they receive from others.

| Pattern IV | | |
|---|---|---|
| **Lead Strengths** | **Supporting Strengths** | **Flex-patterns** |
| Thinking | Risking | VIII |
| Theoretical thinking | Practical thinking | II |
| Independent risking | Dependent risking | III |

## Relationship Strengths

People who have Pattern IV strengths are the most introverted of all the eight patterns. All three lead strengths of this pattern point inward: thinking, theoretical thinking, and independence. The combination of these three strengths results in a creative and innovative thinker. One of the most important contributions Pattern IVs make to their relationships is to bring in new ideas and innovative approaches to solving old problems.

They tend to be leaders in the realm of new ideas and innovations, but normally they are not leaders of people in the emotional sense. They tend to follow ideas that are either their own, or the ideas of others that they have thought through and made their own. They usually express their leadership most effectively in writing and are less effective in face-to-face activities such as debating.

Those with Pattern IV strengths can bring other values to their relationships by deliberately emphasizing their three supporting strengths. First, they can make the relationship more dynamic and exciting by emphasizing their assertive strengths (Flex-pattern VIII). Second, they can bring in more realism by emphasizing their practical thinking (Flex-pattern II). Third, they can inject more warmth and appreciation into the relationship by emphasizing their dependent strength (Flex-pattern III).

## Natural Tendencies

People who have Pattern IV strengths are characteristically reserved and independent in their relationships. Their major tendency is to withdraw into their own self-sufficiency and work out their problems alone. Expression of this tendency can make others feel rejected, left out, and depreciated.

Another tendency that frequently gives them a problem in their relationships is their tendency toward perfection. This causes them to be overly critical and demanding of other people, thus putting people on the defensive and driving them away.

Still another problem they sometimes experience in their relationships comes from their tendency to become married to their own ideas. They feel personally threatened if anyone questions or belittles their ideas. They tend to reject those who don't appreciate their ideas and can become very critical of them.

## What Those with Pattern IV Strengths Want From Others

The most important thing people with Pattern IV strengths want from others is respect. They value their autonomy very highly and are supersensitive to violations of their territory. Although they want and need relationships with others, it is important that they have space and distance in these relationships.

They want to be independent and self-sufficient and want others to be the same in their relationships with them. The most difficult thing for IVs to handle in a relationship is an expression of dependence. They have difficulty expressing their own dependence and tend to feel restricted and violated when others depend too heavily on them.

They feel threatened when others try to get too close or personal. They feel very uncomfortable when others push too hard, demanding an emotional reaction from them. They want respect, but they are easily embarrassed if they are put in the limelight. They usually feel awkward in accepting compliments.

## Pᴀᴛᴛᴇʀɴ V

| Lead Strengths | Supporting Strengths | Flex-patterns |
|---|---|---|
| Risking | Thinking | I |
| Practical thinking | Theoretical thinking | VI |
| Dependent risking | Independent risking | VII |

## Relationship Strengths

Pattern V strengths tend to produce people who are very extra-verted. Their three lead strengths are risking, dependence, and prac-tical thinking. All of these are outer-directed strengths. Relationships with others are most important of all for people who have this combination of strengths. They are assertive in establishing relation-ships and continually seek closeness with other people. Although all people need and want the warmth of human companionships, with Pattern Vs, interaction with other people is at the center of their lives. All other values are secondary.

People with these strengths are usually very much aware of other people—especially of their feelings. They are very interested in the per-sonal lives of other people and invite others to share their feelings. It is very easy to talk to Pattern Vs. Networking is second nature to them.

They are usually good coordinators of practical affairs. It is easy and natural for them to express affection, warmth, and acceptance (which is the natural emotional bridge for commu-nication). Generally speaking, Vs are excellent communicators. Frequently they are highly effective as one-to-one counselors.

Those who have Pattern V strengths can bring other values to their relationships by deliberately emphasizing their three supporting strengths. First, they can bring in rationality and reserve by emphasizing their thinking strengths (Flex-pattern I). Second, they can bring dynamic leadership to the relationship by empha-sizing their independent strength (Flex-pattern VII). Third, they can bring in a vision of possibilities by emphasizing their imaginative strengths (Flex-pattern VI).

## Natural Tendencies

People who have the Pattern V strengths are naturally assertive and relational in their relationships. One of their strongest tendencies is to go overboard in pleasing other people. Sometimes this causes them to get so involved in helping others they find they have no time for themselves. They find their lives ruled by the wants, needs, and demands of others. They are no longer running their own lives.

They live on recognition and compliments. In an effort to be well liked and approved by others, they sometimes avoid confrontation and conflict when they should stand up for their own rights. One of their most troublesome tendencies is to say "yes" when they should say "no."

## What Those with Pattern V Strengths Want From Others

Pattern Vs want others to react to them—to show their feelings and say what they are thinking. They especially want others to tell them how they are feeling toward them. It is not enough to tell Pattern Vs how you feel about them only occasionally. They want you to tell them every day.

When they make an overture of friendliness, they want a response! They much prefer a warm friendly response, but even bad news is better than no news at all. They want to be noticed and recognized. It is hard to give them too many compliments.

People with Pattern V strengths want to be needed. They want others to ask for their help and accept what they have to give. Their greatest fulfillment comes when they are doing something for someone else.

**Pattern VI**

| Lead Strengths | Supporting Strengths | Flex-patterns |
|---|---|---|
| Risking | Thinking | III |
| Theoretical thinking | Practical thinking | V |
| Dependent risking | Independent risking | VIII |

## Relationship Strengths

People who have Pattern VI strengths bring a good deal of emotional warmth to a relationship. Their outgoing, people-oriented strengths are frequently expressed in an easy social grace that makes others feel warm and accepted. Their emotional feel for people and situations helps to lubricate human relationships and bring people closer together.

They initiate communication and bring a dynamic spark to a relationship. They like to see people happy and having a good time. They like to entertain and please other people. VIs have the natural strengths that contribute life, sparkle, and warmth to group activities.

Those who have Pattern VI strengths can bring other values to their relationships by deliberately emphasizing their three supporting strengths. First, they can bring rationality by emphasizing their thinking strengths (Flex-pattern III). Second, they can bring dynamic leadership by emphasizing their strength of independence (Flex-pattern VIII). Third, they can bring practicality to the relationship by emphasizing their practical thinking strength (Flex-pattern V).

## Natural Tendencies

People who have Pattern VI strengths are naturally assertive and relational in their relationships. The tendency that probably gives them most problems is that of going overboard to please other people. They can get so involved in making other people happy that they can't say "no" to them when it needs to be said. Thus, they can arrive at the point where the needs and demands of others are ruling their lives.

Another tendency that sometimes gives them a problem is trusting people too much. They have the tendency to trust and idealize people beyond the reality of their trustworthiness. As a result, other people can easily take advantage of them.

Their tendency to come on too strong and smother the other person with excessive attention, concern, and affection can also cause major problems in their relationships. Usually this causes the other person to run away, reject, or attack them. Any of these responses is distressing to the Pattern VI.

## What Those with Pattern VI Strengths Want From Others

How other people relate to them is of critical importance to those who have Pattern VI strengths. Relationships with others are important to everyone, but with them, it is the most important single force in their lives. Since relationships are so critically important to them, they are highly sensitive to the quality of their relationships and tend to be affected greatly by them.

They want to be needed. They want others to ask them for their help and trust them to be a friend. They want others to be open with their feelings and share their problems with them.

They want to be recognized and appreciated in very obvious ways. They want others to tell them how much they appreciate them and lay it on heavy. They don't want to guess how other people are feeling toward them—they want to be told!

They want other people to interact with them in a warm and accepting way. Perhaps their greatest enjoyment comes when other people respond to them in an active way, displaying a good deal of warm appreciation and sincere friendliness.

## Pattern VII

| Lead Strengths | Supporting Strengths | Flex-patterns |
|---|---|---|
| Risking | Thinking | II |
| Practical thinking | Theoretical thinking | VIII |
| Independent risking | Dependent risking | V |

## Relationship Strengths

People who have Pattern VII strengths bring initiative, confidence, enthusiasm, and dynamic movement to a relationship. They stimulate action and get things moving. They are natural emotional leaders who step out front and say, "Follow me."

They energize a relationship. They bring a high drive to accomplish and a full dedication to winning. They bring the excitement of competitive challenge and the courage to move and do, in spite of the risk. The quote from an early American naval hero, "Damn the torpedoes, full speed ahead," is very descriptive of the leadership and courage they can bring to their relationships.

Practicality is another strength people with Pattern VII strengths bring to a relationship. They risk on a calculated basis and are realistic about what can be accomplished. They encourage others to seek out practical ways to accomplish their objectives.

Those who have Pattern VII strengths can bring other values to their relationships by consciously emphasizing their three supporting strengths. First, they can bring in more rationality and planning by emphasizing their thinking strengths (Flex-pattern II). Second, they can bring in more warm encouragement and support by emphasizing their dependent strengths (Flex-pattern V). Third, they can bring in more vision of possibilities by emphasizing their theoretical thinking strength (Flex-pattern VIII).

## Natural Tendencies

People who have Pattern VII strengths are naturally assertive and independent in their relationships. They tend to move assertively into other people's territory and sometimes move right on past others as they actively pursue their personal goals.

Because of their high drive to accomplish, Pattern VIIs tend to experience a good deal of impatience with other people. They usually have clear and compelling goals they want to accomplish, and they quickly become impatient with anything that interferes with or slows down the process of achieving them. They tend to be much more aware of what they are trying to accomplish than they are of the other person in the relationship.

They also have a strong tendency to talk when they should be listening. Frequently, when they are not saying anything in a relationship, they are not really listening but are figuring out what they are going to say when the other person stops talking.

## What Those with Pattern VII Strengths Want From Others

Those with Pattern VII strengths want an active relationship where there is a lot of excitement and give-and-take going on. They want a response more than anything else. The kind of response is not too important—they simply want a response.

They want people to come on direct and straightforward, saying what they mean, and with force. They enjoy others being competitive, even to the point of conflict. Sometimes a good fight is just what they want.

They want recognition, and they enjoy being in the spotlight. They want to be leaders and have others follow them. They want the relationship to be productive and accomplish something.

### PATTERN VIII

| Lead Strengths | Supporting Strengths | Flex-patterns |
|---|---|---|
| Risking | Thinking | IV |
| Theoretical thinking | Practical thinking | VII |
| Independent risking | Dependent risking | VI |

## Relationship Strengths

People who have Pattern VIII strengths bring excitement, enthusiasm, confidence, and imagination to their relationships. They fire people's imaginations and stir their emotions. They are emotional leaders who sell and promote their ideas and dreams. Many political and religious leaders have Pattern VIII strengths.

They take the initiative in their relationships. They willingly make the first move and get the interaction started. If the relationship becomes dull and boring, they find ways to liven it up. They step out front, take a strong position, and expose themselves on their own initiative. They contribute energy, spontaneity, and dynamic action—things happen in their relationships.

They can bring other values into their relationships by consciously emphasizing their three supporting strengths. First, they can bring more rationality and stability into the relationship by shifting to their Flex-pattern IV and emphasizing their thinking strengths. Second, they can inject warm encouragement and support by shifting to their Flex-pattern VI and emphasizing their dependent strengths. Third, they can bring in realism and practicality by shifting to their Flex-pattern VII and emphasizing their practical thinking strengths.

## Natural Tendencies

Those who have Pattern VIII strengths are naturally assertive and independent in their relationships. One of their most obvious tendencies is to move assertively toward other people and seek to have a strong impact on them. In their efforts to strongly influence others, they frequently overstate, exaggerate, and make extreme statements. Sometimes they take an extreme position in order to shock people and draw attention to themselves.

They tend to talk when they should be listening. Their normal orientation tends to make them so intent on influencing others that they don't have time to be influenced themselves. Sometimes, others give up and leave the relationship because they find it so difficult to influence the Pattern VIII.

Another tendency that sometimes gives them problems in their relationships is taking action too quickly—before they get all the facts. Although their intuitive feel is very valuable and sometimes very accurate, in the absence of a solid rational basis, their actions become suspect to most people.

## What Those with Pattern VIII Strengths Want From Others

Those with Pattern VIII strengths want the spotlight. They like to be highly visible and noticed by other people. They want others to recognize them and respond to their leadership.

They want to see the impact they are having on others. They want others to show them how they are being influenced. The most difficult thing for them to handle is a non-response. A person who just sits there and refuses to interact is an enigma for them. Without some response, they have no place to go— they don't know what to do next to try to influence the person.

They want other people to be influenced strongly by them and to interact with them based on that influence. They want to maintain control of the relationship and have it focus on their own interest and concerns.

# 13

# How to Strengthen Relationships

The three sections of this chapter present some practical guidelines for using the Power of Opposite Strengths to strengthen relationships.

The first section discusses how we can deal creatively with our natural tendencies when they give us problems in our relationships. It shows how we can blend in a stronger expression of our supporting strengths, yet still remain true to our natural way of being.

The second section gives some practical suggestions on how we can discover another person's natural pattern of strengths.

The third section explores how we can strengthen our relationships by relating to other people in terms of their own natural patterns.

A chart at the end of the chapter gives some specific suggestions on how to relate to other individuals based upon their particular patterns of strengths.

## Dealing Creatively With Our Own Relationship Tendencies

In the previous discussion on personal growth, mature people were described as those who do two things well. First, they are true to themselves: They express their natural way of being. Second, they are flexible and adaptable: They emphasize their supporting strengths when the situation requires it. The same creative duality operates in people who develop strong relationships with others.

First, they show who they really are by expressing their natural way of being. Second, they deliberately shift emphasis to their supporting strengths when the relationship requires it. It is important to emphasize that they do both of these things. Although doing these two seemingly opposite things may appear to be a paradox, this is precisely what people do when they have a creative and productive relationship with another person. They show their true nature and, at the same time, express the strengths needed to build up the relationship.

Figure 17 illustrates how we can, in actual practice, remain true to our natural way of being, and, at the same time, consciously blend in a stronger expression of our supporting strengths. The four diagrams in Figure 17 are the same ones used in Figure 16 to depict how the four relationship tendencies are expressed in our relationships. A dashed arrow has been added in each of the four diagrams, however, to show how we can move into the zone of sustained success with another person by keeping our natural way of being and emphasizing our supporting strengths at the same time.

The diagram at the top of Figure 17 shows how a person who tends to be reserved and relational can move into the zone of sustained success by being a little more assertive and independent in the relationship. Those who have natural patterns I or III tend to experience this tendency the most. The dashed arrow goes closer to the Line of Sustained Success and moves closer to the horizontal. This indicates more assertiveness and more equality in the relationship. The dashed arrow is still back from the Line of Sustained Success and still droops down somewhat, but not as much as before. In this way, the person still shows the characteristics of reserve and dependence, but at the same time blends in a stronger expression of assertiveness and independence. Dealing with a reserved and relational tendency in this way creates the best opportunity to strengthen relationships with other people.

# Dealing Creatively With Our Relationship Tendencies

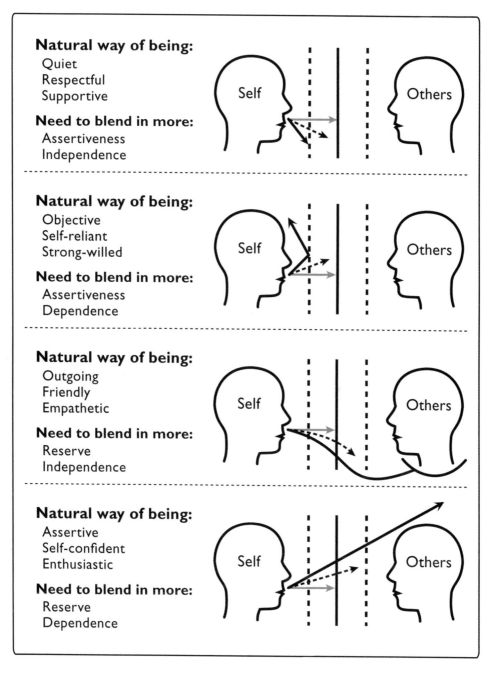

**Natural way of being:**
Quiet
Respectful
Supportive

**Need to blend in more:**
Assertiveness
Independence

Self          Others

**Natural way of being:**
Objective
Self-reliant
Strong-willed

**Need to blend in more:**
Assertiveness
Dependence

Self          Others

**Natural way of being:**
Outgoing
Friendly
Empathetic

**Need to blend in more:**
Reserve
Independence

Self          Others

**Natural way of being:**
Assertive
Self-confident
Enthusiastic

**Need to blend in more:**
Reserve
Dependence

Self          Others

*Figure 17*

The second diagram illustrates how those with the reserved and independent tendency can blend in more assertiveness and dependence, thereby strengthening their relationships. Those with natural patterns II and IV tend to experience this tendency. The dashed arrow shows that their natural way of being is still there but is modified to a degree by their being somewhat more assertive and dependent. The arrow moves closer to the Line of Sustained Success and moves down somewhat, indicating a more level relationship with the other person. In actual behavior, they show more awareness and concern for others and move closer to them. Those who have this tendency still show the flavor of reserve and independence, but they make a conscious, obvious effort to be more assertive and dependent.

The third diagram illustrates how those with assertive and relational tendencies can blend in more reserve and independence, thereby building stronger relationships. Those with natural patterns V or VI tend to experience this tendency. As indicated by the dashed arrow, those with this tendency still express their natural assertiveness and warmth toward the other person, but they moderate the expression of these strengths by blending in more thinking and self-sufficiency. In actual behavior, they become more thoughtful and depend more on their own internal strengths to solve their problems. Their natural warmth and caring for others is still there and functional, but it is expressed with more respect for others and in a quieter way.

The fourth diagram at the bottom of Figure 17 illustrates how those with assertive and independent tendencies can modify their expression of these strengths and create stronger relationships with others. Those with natural patterns VII or VIII tend to express this tendency. The dashed arrow indicates that those who have this tendency become more thoughtful and reserved, and they focus their attention more on the other person in the relationship.

Their natural assertiveness and self-confidence is still there, but it is made more creative by a stronger blend of basic thinking and courage to depend more on the other person.

# Knowing the Other Person

In our efforts to strengthen a relationship, it is important that we understand ourselves, and it is equally important that we understand the other person in the relationship. The Power of Opposite Strengths can be used to deepen our understanding of another person and, based upon that understanding, to strengthen the relationship. Our knowledge of a person's natural pattern of strengths gives us dependable guidelines for what we must do to build a strong relationship and good communication with that person.

How can we go about discovering other people's natural patterns of strengths? There are at least three distinct avenues we may pursue. First, we can use the results of the *Opposite Strength Inventories*. Second, we can talk with them about their own perceptions of their natural pattern of strengths. Third, we can observe them and make subjective guesses about their patterns.

## Using the Results of the *Opposite Strengths Inventories*

The most reliable and valid way for an individual to accurately identify his or her natural pattern of strengths is to use the *Opposite Strengths Inventories* along with the experience of attending an Opposite Strengths Seminar or being coached by an Opposite Strengths Certified Executive Coach. The fact that you are reading this book indicates that you are probably doing just that. Our Web site (*www.oppositestrengths.com*) is also a rich resource. In addition to making our Inventories and our three in-depth reports (the *Guide to Being Yourself, Guide to Being Flexible,* and *Relationship Guide*) available online, it provides a primer on the Power of Opposite Strengths, along with additional stand-alone and supplemental activities.

People who have the experience of an Opposite Strengths Seminar or Opposite Strengths Executive Coaching are the most successful in strengthening their relationships using the Power of Opposite Strengths. They fully understand their natural patterns of strengths, and they speak a common language regarding relationships.

## Talking With Other People about Their Natural Patterns

Beyond just observing and thinking about others, we can gather additional information directly. We can engage them in a discussion of the Power of Opposite Strengths and ask what they see as their natural pattern of strengths. An interaction of this sort is usually a very satisfying and productive experience for both parties. Frequently, it results in getting to know others much better, and we usually end up having a much better idea about their natural patterns.

If the other person has not been through the experience of an Opposite Strengths Seminar or Opposite Strengths Executive Coaching, however, that lack of background knowledge and experience will limit the full benefits of knowing the natural patterns.

## Making a Subjective Guess about another Person's Natural Pattern

As we observe the personality characteristics displayed by other people, we can begin to associate them with particular patterns. For example, if a person tends to be quiet and reserved, it suggests a lead strength in thinking. A good guess, therefore, is that his or her natural pattern is I, II, III, or IV. If, on the other hand, the person is active, outgoing, and assertive, it would suggest one of the risking patterns—V, VI, VII, or VIII. As we observe other characteristics being expressed, we will pick up additional clues that suggest a leaning toward a particular strength. When we have enough information, we make an educated guess regarding the person's basic pattern. Then we look for evidence to either confirm that pattern or call it into question.

There are at least five important limitations to this approach. The first is that the knowledge of the patterns and all that is behind them cannot be freely shared between the two people in the relationship. The second is that the tendency is to type that individual and box him or her in rather than considering all of the characteristics and facets that make a person who he or she is. The third is that one person's perception of another is subject to all kinds of factors that produce inaccurate perceptions of the other person (most importantly, the ongoing relationship with that person). The fourth is that if we have only a superficial understanding of the patterns, our guesses are not very educated. Our own needs, desires, and prejudices constitute a fifth factor that also influences the accuracy of our guess regarding another person's pattern. Our perception of another person's natural pattern is always distorted to some degree by our own wants. We can very easily perceive people as we want them to be rather than as who they are in reality.

The best way to develop an understanding of someone else's natural pattern of strengths is to ask that person to attend an Opposite Strengths Seminar or to engage an Opposite Strengths Certified Executive Coach.

# Relating to Others in Terms of Their Natural Patterns of Strengths

Being aware of other people's natural patterns of strengths gives us some valuable information regarding how we can go about strengthening our relationships with them. Figure 5 presents some specific suggestions about how to be most effective in our relationships with people when we know their patterns of strengths.

That said, everyone should keep in mind that the pattern is a conceptual tool to help us understand ourselves and other people. People are affected by four life forces, and the natural pattern of strengths is only one of them. (To review information on the four life forces, see Part I).

The best way to develop a good understanding of your relationship with someone else is to go to our Web site and produce a *Relationship Guide* for the two of you. Below, you can find out how.

# Applying Opposite Strengths in Your Life

Return to the Web site (*www.oppositestrengths.com*) to generate a *Relationship Guide*.

At the end of Part II, you probably visited our Web site, and generated your *Guide to Being Flexible*. Your *Guide to Being Flexible* discussed your three flex-patterns in detail and gave you guidance on how to become a more effective person—how to create a better relationship with yourself.

Now it is time for you to generate a *Relationship Guide*. You can see a sample *Relationship Guide* on your Member Home Page. Just click the link "*Relationship Guide*" under the heading "Sample reports."

You can produce a *Relationship Guide* that applies to you and any other member of our Web site, provided that the other member has at least one completed *Inventory* (either a Self- or an Other-report) that has previously been included in a *Guide*.

Since you may generate as many *Relationship Guides* as you wish, you can potentially develop a better understanding of your relationships with many of the people who are significant in your life.

Follow these easy steps to produce a *Relationship Guide* online.

- Use your Member ID (e-mail address) and Password to log on to your Member Home Page at *www.oppositestrengths.com*.

- Under the heading "Opposite Strengths Reports," click on the link "*Relationship Guide*."

- Either choose the name of the person from the drop down list or, if that person is not listed, enter the Member

ID (e-mail address) of the other person you want to have included in the *Relationship Guide* along with you. Click "Go."

Your *Relationship Guide* with that other person will immediately appear!

In closing, I want to thank you for reading this book. I hope you have learned a great deal and that you are successfully applying that knowledge in your daily life and your relationships.

—Dr. Tommy Thomas

# Transition

Now you have finished reading the book. You may still be engaged in Opposite Strengths Executive Coaching or have attended an Opposite Strengths Seminar or both. Hopefully, you have generated all three of you online *Guides*. You are on your way to realizing the Power of Opposite Strengths!

We offer the Opposite Strengths Seminar described in this book to organizations throughout the world. We also train and certify new Opposite Strengths Certified Facilitators in these organizations. We also welcome seasoned executive coaches to join our global community of Opposite Strengths Certified Executive Coaches through our Web site. Opposite Strengths Certified Executive Coaches live in many parts of the world, and our expansion into languages other than American English is getting under way (See details on our Web site.)

We invite you to contact us with your interests and questions. Sign up for our monthly newsletter on *www.oppositestrengths.com*. But most of all, use Opposite Strengths to sustain your success in both your personal and professional lives!

# Partial List of Clients

For a complete listing of our over 1,300 client organizations, please visit our Web site at *www.oppositestrengths.com*. Click the "Our clients" link to see a list of all the organizations that have used the Power of Opposite Strengths since 1966.

| Client | City | State/Province | Country |
|---|---|---|---|
| American Electronics Association | Colorado Springs | Colorado | United States |
| Budget Rent-A-Car | Lisle | Illinois | United States |
| Canadian Red Cross Society | Toronto | Ontario | Canada |
| Day-Timers, Inc. | East Texas | Pennsylvania | United States |
| Ernst & Young | New York City | New York | United States |
| Foxboro Great Britain Ltd. | Redhill | Surrey | England |
| Grupo Anastasis | Mexico City | Districto Federal | Mexico |
| Hockey Alberta | Red Deer | Alberta | Canada |
| IBM | Austin | Texas | United States |
| Lucent Technologies | Santa Barbara | California | United States |
| Methodist Hospital Foundation | Jacksonville | Florida | United States |
| Nordstrom | San Diego | California | United States |
| Oklahoma State University | Stillwater | Oklahoma | United States |
| Perkin-Elmer | Danbury | Connecticut | United States |
| Poudre Valley Health System | Fort Collins | Colorado | United States |
| Queensway Baptist Church | Brantford | Ontario | Canada |
| River Oaks Bank & Trust Co. | Houston | Texas | United States |
| Schumpert Medical Center | Shreveport | Louisiana | United States |

| Client | City | State/Province | Country |
|---|---|---|---|
| Texas Instruments | Dallas | Texas | United States |
| U. S. Navy | Norfolk | Virginia | United States |
| Victoria's Secret | Columbus | Ohio | United States |
| World Bank | Washington | District of Columbia | United States |
| YMCA | Newport | Rhode Island | United States |
| ZymoGenetics | Seattle | Washington | United States |

# About the Authors

T. J. (Tommy) Thomas is an educational psychologist with over 30 years of experience leading Opposite Strengths Seminars, coaching top executives using Opposite Strengths Executive Coaching, training the executive coaches and facilitators who use Opposite Strengths with others, coordinating research on the Power of Opposite Strengths, and consulting with client organizations.

He conducted extensive research on the *Opposite Strengths Inventories* in his 1982 doctoral dissertation. He has contributed to the development of seminars and other publications on the Power of Opposite Strengths since the early 1980's. He is currently writing more books applying the Power of Opposite Strengths to executive coaching and organizational productivity and cultural transformation issues.

Dr. Thomas attended the University of Texas at Austin. He received his Bachelor's degree in Plan II (an honors liberal arts program) in 1973 and his Doctor of Philosophy degree in psychometrics and educational psychology in 1982.

Dr. Thomas conducts Opposite Strengths Seminars for clients and develops new products using the Power of Opposite Strengths. As CEO of Opposite Strengths, Inc., he takes an active role in developing the Power of Opposite Strengths Web site to be a leader in providing online coaching and positive human development on the Internet. He is a Licensed Psychologist in the State of Texas.

J. W. (Jay) Thomas is a management psychologist with over 50 years of experience consulting with and coaching management people in business and education. He is the originator of the Power of Opposite Strengths and has been working on its development since 1961.

He wrote the original book on the Power of Opposite Strengths in 1971. He is the primary developer of the *Opposite Strengths Inventories* and the *Analysis of Strengths*. He created many seminars used in organizations to put the Power of Opposite Strengths to practical use.

Dr. Thomas attended Stanford University and Southern Methodist University before earning his Bachelor's degree in mathematics and philosophy at Oklahoma State University. He earned his Master's and Doctor of Education degrees in psychology and education at Oklahoma State University.

Born in 1917, Dr. Thomas remains active writing about the Power of Opposite Strengths. When he was active consulting with clients, Dr. Thomas was a Licensed Psychologist in the State of Texas.

# Index

## Symbols

*7 Habits of Highly Effective People*, 52
360 Degree Feedback, 79

## A

*Analysis of Strengths*, xiv, 78, 79, 112, 233
assertive and independent tendency, 191, 198, 200
assertive and relational tendency, 191, 197
attitude of equality, 11, 182, 183

## B

basic pair, 41, 117
basic strength, 140
behaviorism, 2
being assertive, 12, 183
being flexible, 9, 156, 158, 160, 162, 164, 166, 168, 170
being reserved, 12
being respectful, 183
being true to oneself, 150, 156, 158, 160, 162, 164, 166, 168, 170
being true to the situation, 151
being yourself, 7
bipolar, ix, x
Bi/Polar, ix, 64

## C

Carter, Jimmy, 73
Certified Executive Coaches, xiv, 76, 78, 79
Certified Facilitator, xiv, 78, 79, 110
client organizations, 230
Collins, Jim, 48

common language, xiii
common tendencies, 131, 132, 140
Copernicus, 73
courage, 42
Covey, Stephen, 52

## D

Darwin, Charles, 73
DaVinci, Leonardo, 73
DeGaulle, Charles, 74
dependent risking, 39, 49, 50, 52, 57, 138, 146, 193, 195
DiSC, 1

## E

Earhart, Amelia, 74
Einstein, Albert, 73
Eisenhower, Dwight D., 73
emotion, 41
environment, 27, 32, 95, 97, 101, 102, 103

## F

father-son relationships, 186
Fifth Principle, 17
First Principle, 16
Fitzgerald, F. Scott, 13
five principles, 37
flexibility, 117, 152
Flex-pattern I, 210
Flex-pattern II, 156, 214
Flex-pattern III, 163, 167, 212
Flex-pattern IV, 170, 206
flex-patterns, 76, 150, 151, 152
Flex-pattern V, 169, 202
Flex-pattern VI, 160, 211

Flex-pattern VII, 158, 164, 216
Flex-pattern VIII, 208
four life forces, 27, 101
Fourth Principle, 17

**G**

Gardner, Howard, 93
Good to Great, 48
growth process, 117, 118, 122, 148, 153
*Guide to Being Flexible*, xiv, 79, 112, 175, 176, 223, 227
*Guide to Being Yourself*, xiv, 79, 110, 112, 175, 223

**I**

iceberg analogy, 2
independent risking, 39, 49, 50, 57, 121, 138, 146, 195, 197, 199
infinity symbol, 56
innate capacities, 27, 29, 32, 35, 91, 94
insight, 1, 16
interdependence, 53

**J**

Johnson, Lyndon B., 74

**K**

Kaufman Assessment Battery for Children, 93
Kennedy, Jack, 73
King, Martin Luther, 74

**L**

lead strength, 43, 44, 48, 53, 57
learned tendency, 129, 130

Line of Sustained Success, 173, 174, 184, 185, 187, 188, 189, 193, 220

**M**

*Manual for the Bi/Polar Inventory of Strengths*, 39
Mayo, Clyde, 78
Member Home Page, 79, 110, 112, 175, 227
Member ID, 112, 175, 227
Member Password, 112, 175
multiple intelligences, 93
Myers-Briggs Type Indicator, 1

**N**

natural pattern of strengths, 59, 74
natural tendencies, 129, 131, 202, 204, 207, 208, 211, 215, 216

**O**

*Opposite Strength Inventories*, 91, 223
Opposite Strengths, 229, 232
Opposite Strengths Certified Executive Coach, 110, 223, 225
Opposite Strengths Certified Executive Coach Community, xi, xv
Opposite Strengths Certified Executive Coaches, 229
Opposite Strengths Certified Facilitator, 110, 229
Opposite Strengths Culture Transformation, xiii, 176
Opposite Strengths Executive Coaching, xiii, xiv, 110, 112, 176, 224, 229, 232
Opposite Strengths Executive Coaching System, xv
Opposite Strengths Inventories, xiv,

76, 77, 78, 79, 80, 110, 175, 232, 233
Opposite Strengths Seminar, xiii,
xiv, 5, 6, 13, 45, 80, 109, 110, 112,
175, 176, 223, 224, 225, 229, 232
Opposite Strengths System, xi, xiv,
6, 9, 13

**P**

Password, 227
Pattern I, 59, 60, 73, 82, 156, 157,
202, 203
Pattern II, 59, 61, 66, 73, 83, 158,
159, 194, 204, 205
Pattern III, 62, 73, 84, 160, 161, 206,
207
Pattern IV, 62, 64, 66, 73, 85, 162,
163, 194, 209
Patterns I and III, 192
patterns of strengths, 27, 29, 30, 31,
32, 37, 38, 53, 94
Pattern V, 67, 68, 73, 86, 164, 197,
210, 211
Pattern VI, 67, 68, 74, 87, 166, 167,
197, 212, 213
Pattern VII, 69, 70, 74, 88, 169, 199,
214, 215
Pattern VIII, 69, 70, 74, 89, 170, 171,
199, 216, 217
Patton, George, 74
perfect relationship, 183
personal choice, 27, 29, 34, 95, 102,
103, 107, 108, 109
personal growth, 118, 124, 149, 153,
154
personality, 27, 95, 97, 104
personality development, 105, 108,
117
personal operating system, 3
personal tendency, 129, 155

polarization, 133, 135, 137, 139, 140,
149
Power of Opposite Strengths, ix,
x, xiii, xiv, 1, 3, 5, 6, 8, 10, 16, 20,
25, 26, 29, 31, 33, 34, 37, 43, 45, 47,
49, 50, 57, 59, 77, 78, 91, 92, 93, 94,
98, 101, 103, 104, 108, 113, 117, 121,
123, 124, 125, 126, 131, 135, 136,
138, 149, 173, 181, 192, 219, 224,
229, 230, 232, 233
practical thinking, 39, 46, 48, 56, 93,
118, 136, 142, 145
president, 14
productivity, 3, 4
psychological decay, 137, 149

**R**

relationship, 10, 113, 177, 181
relationship dynamics, 181
*Relationship Guide*, xiv, 79, 80, 176,
177, 224, 226, 227, 228
relationships, 1
relationship strengths, 202, 204,
206, 208, 210, 212, 214, 216
relationship tendencies, 177, 191,
221
relationship with oneself, 150
reserved and independent tendency,
191, 193, 194
reserved and relational tendency,
191, 192
risking, 18, 39, 41, 42, 45, 56, 117,
195, 199
risking pair, 49, 118
risking strength, 42, 145
Rogers, Will, 74
Roosevelt, Franklin D., 74
Roosevelt, Theodore, 74

## S

Saint Paul, 74
Second Principle, 16
*Self-Other Agreement as Manifested by Differential Responses on Self-Report and Other-Report Forms of Personality Inventories*, 39
Senge, Peter, 1
Sixth Principle, 19
Skinner, B. F., 2
Sperry, Roger, 93
Stockdale Paradox, 48
strengthen relationships, 219
strengths, x, 3, 15, 19, 26, 30
supervisor-subordinate relationships, 187
Sustained Success, 10
*Sustaining Your Success Pocket Guide*, 80

## T

tendencies, 129
*The Courage to Be*, 41, 49
theoretical thinking, 39, 46, 48, 56, 118, 145
thinking, 18, 39, 41, 42, 45, 56, 117, 193, 195
thinking pair, 46, 118
thinking strength, 42, 142, 197
Third Principle, 17
Thomas, Jay, x, 13, 41, 47, 49, 64, 78, 102, 117, 125, 126, 233
Thomas, Tommy, x, xiii, 21, 39, 112, 176, 228, 232
Thoreau, 73
three pairs of strengths, 39
Tillich, Paul, 41, 49
Truman, Harry S., 73
Twain, Mark, 74

## W

weakness, 26, 120
Wilson, Woodrow, 73
www.oppositestrengths.com, 5, 79, 80, 110, 112, 175, 223, 227, 229, 230

## Z

zone of sustained success, 188, 189